H. Tennant

Laws Regulating the Relative Rights and Duties of Masters, Servants, and Apprentices in the Cape Colony

Annotated with Decisions under the Different Sections

H. Tennant

Laws Regulating the Relative Rights and Duties of Masters, Servants, and Apprentices in the Cape Colony
Annotated with Decisions under the Different Sections

ISBN/EAN: 9783337232290

Printed in Europe, USA, Canada, Australia, Japan

Cover: Foto ©Suzi / pixelio.de

More available books at **www.hansebooks.com**

LAWS

REGULATING THE RELATIVE

RIGHTS AND DUTIES

OF

MASTERS, SERVANTS,

AND

APPRENTICES

IN THE

CAPE COLONY.

ANNOTATED WITH DECISIONS UNDER THE DIFFERENT SECTIONS.

BY

H. TENNANT,

OF THE INNER TEMPLE, BARRISTER-AT-LAW.

Editor of "The Rules of Court," "Notary's Manual," etc., etc.

CAPE TOWN: J. C. JUTA & CO.

1890.

LONDON:
PRINTED BY WILLIAM CLOWES AND SONS, Limited,
STAMFORD STREET AND CHARING CROSS.

PREFACE.

The following pages are published in order to meet the desire, often expressed by many members of the community, for a convenient and easy reference to the Masters' and Servants' Laws of the Colony.

H. T.

CHAMBERS, *January*, 1890.

Contracts entered into in England.

The following important case was decided by the Supreme Court on the 3rd of March last, after this pamphlet had passed through the Press :—

SAYERS vs. THORNE.

This was an appeal from a decision of the Resident Magistrate of Cape Town on a case in which the appellant was charged with having failed to perform a contract made by her in England to enter the service of the respondent in Cape Town as a cook, and with respect to which it was contended for the appellant that the contract was not executed in accordance with the terms of the Act. The objection was overruled, and the appellant was sentenced to pay a fine of £2, or to undergo a month's imprisonment. Mr. Innes now appeared in support of the appeal, and Mr. Giddy for the respondent.

Mr. Innes contended that the conviction was bad, because section 10 of sub-section 1 of Act No. 1 of 1873 provided that contracts of service in which it was not stipulated that the service was to commence within a month were not binding unless executed before a magistrate or some officer specially appointed for that purpose. He held that this section repealed section 1 of Act No. 15 of 1856. In this case the contract was made in Southampton, but it was not made before a magistrate or other officer who held an appointment from the Government of the Colony.

Counsel having been heard,

The Chief Justice held that if there was any ambiguity in construing an Act of this kind, the Court must look at the whole Act, and at the enactments it was intended to modify. His opinion was that the Legislature, in framing the Act of 1873, intended it to apply to contracts entered into in the Colony, and that the proviso that certain contracts of service should be entered into before a magistrate applied wholly to magistrates in the Colony. It could never have been the intention of the Legislature that, when an employer had paid the passage of a servant to the Colony, the servant on arriving here should have the power of refusing to enter the service. He thought the Court ought not to disturb the finding of the Magistrate, and that the appeal ought to be dismissed.

MASTERS AND SERVANTS.

No. 15—1856.] AN ACT [June 4, 1856. Act 15—185

To Amend the Laws regulating the relative Rights and Duties of Masters, Servants, and Apprentices.

Preamble.

Whereas it is expedient to amend and consolidate the laws regulating the relative rights and duties of masters, servants, and apprentices: Be it therefore enacted by the Governor of the Cape of Good Hope, with the advice and consent of the Legislative Council and the House of Assembly thereof, as follows:

Repugnant laws repealed.

1. From and after the commencement and taking effect of this Act, the Ordinance entituled " An Ordinance for amending and consolidating the Laws regulating the relative rights and duties of Masters, Servants, and Apprentices," enacted by the Governor of the Cape of Good Hope, with the advice of the Legislative Council thereof, and bearing date the first

B

15—1856. of March, 1841, and all Orders in Council confirming or continuing the said Ordinance (except in so far as the said Ordinance, or any of the said Orders, repeals any former law or usage), the Act No. 4, 1855, entitled " An Act for Encouraging the Importation of European Labourers into this Colony," and all other laws and regulations repugnant to any of the provisions of this Act, shall be repealed, and the same are hereby repealed accordingly.

Interpretation clause.

2. For the purposes and within the meaning of this Act, unless it be otherwise specially provided, or there be something in the subject or in the context repugnant to such construction,—1st, The word "governor" shall mean the officer lawfully administering the government of this colony; 2nd, The word "servant" (I) shall be construed and understood to comprise any person employed for hire, wages, or other remuneration, to perform any handicraft or other bodily labour in agriculture or manufactures, or in domestic service, or as a boatman, porter, or other occupation of a like nature; 3rd, The word "apprentice" shall be construed and understood to comprise any person indentured or bound by any contract of apprenticeship made according to law, as apprentice to any other person; 4th, The word "master" shall be construed and understood to comprise any person, whether male or female, employing for hire, wages, or other remuneration, any person falling within the before-mentioned definition of the word "servant," or to whom any person falling within the before-mentioned definition of the word "apprentice" shall have been indentured or bound by any contract of apprenticeship, made according to law; 5th, The words "contract of service" and "contract of apprenticeship" shall respectively be construed and understood to comprise any agreement, whether oral or written, whether expressed or implied, which any person falling within the before-mentioned definitions of the word "servant" or "apprentice" shall respectively have

---

(1) A stationer's assistant is not a "servant" within the meaning of this section.—*Falconer* v. *Juta*, Buch, 1879, p. 22. *See* also note to § 2, p. 5, *infra*.

entered into or made, according to law, with any person falling ⁴
within the before-mentioned definition of the word "master,"
for .the performance of any work or labour of any kind
hereinbefore mentioned ; 6th, The words "magistrate" and
"magistrates" shall be construed and understood to comprise
the resident magistrates duly appointed for the different
districts of this colony; 7th, The words "this colony" shall
be construed and understood to comprise all islands, and other
territories whatsoever, which are dependent on the colony
of the Cape of Good Hope, and subject to the government
thereof; 8th, The word "month" shall be construed and
understood to comprise the period of one calendar month ;
9th, The words "father," "parent," "relative," "husband,"
and "wife," shall be respectively construed and understood to
comprise reputed fathers, parents, relatives, husbands, or wives,
as well as actual parents and relatives, and lawful husbands
and wives ; 10th, The words "officer" and "proper officer,"
when used with reference to the attestation or making of
contracts of service of apprenticeship, or to the transfer and
assignment of apprentices, shall be construed and understood
to comprise every person who shall have been appointed by
the Governor to attest or make such contracts; 11th, All
words in this Act, and in the various rules and regulations
hereinafter enacted, importing the singular number or the
masculine gender only, shall be construed and understood to
include several persons as well as one person, and females as
well as males.

CHAPTER I.

*In cases not provided for, the law of bilateral contracts in
general to prevail.*

1. Notwithstanding the repeal, by the Ordinance aforesaid,
of the laws thereby repealed, the courts of this colony, in all
cases which are now or shall be hereafter depending before
the same, arising out of or respecting the formation or dissolution of contracts of service or apprenticeship, or touching
or concerning any rights, duties, obligations, powers, liabilities
or other matters or things arising out of or proceeding from

6. any contracts of service or apprenticeship, or any of the mutual relations subsisting between masters and servants or apprentices, shall respectively try, judge, and determine the said causes according to the law of this colony, respecting and applicable to bilateral contracts in general, except when other provisions touching and concerning any such matter and thing as aforesaid shall have been made in this Act, or by any other Law not repealed by the Ordinance aforesaid.

Repeal aforesaid not to annul contracts entered into previously to the taking effect of this Act.

2. The beforementioned repeal shall not annul or affect any contracts of service or apprenticeship entered into previously to the time when this Act shall take effect, and which, under and by virtue of, and according to any laws in force within this colony on the day previously to the taking effect of this Act, were then subsisting legal and valid contracts.

Contracts liable to be set aside on account of fraud, &c.

3. Nevertheless any such last-mentioned contract of service or apprenticeship, to be performed within this colony, shall be liable to be set aside by any magistrate having jurisdiction over the parties, or any competent court, upon reasonable proof being made to the satisfaction of such magistrate or court, that either of the parties to such contract was induced to enter into the same by any fraud, misrepresentation, or concealment.

CHAPTER II.

ON THE FORMATION OF CONTRACTS OF SERVICE.

Contracts entered into out of the colony, how to be certified.

1. No contract of service made elsewhere than within the limits of this colony shall be of force or effect within this colony, except the same shall have been made in writing, and be duly certified by the British consul, or other similar officer, at the place where the same was made, or if there be no such officer, then by such magistrate of such place, or other proper

authority; but contracts not so certified shall, notwithstanding, A
have force and effect in this colony, upon other proof of such
contract, to the satisfaction of the magistrate before whom the
same shall come in question.

Every contract shall be deemed to be entered into for one month,
   unless otherwise specified: except the servant be non-resident,
   or shall work by the piece.

2. Every contract of service, whether oral or written, the
term of endurance of which shall not have been expressly
specified and limited by such contract, shall, in the absence of
sufficient proof to the contrary, be deemed and taken to be for
the term of one month from the commencement thereof; save
and except contracts for service in any trade or handicraft,
whereby it shall not have been stipulated that the servant
shall, during the term thereof, reside in the house of or on the
premises of the master, which shall be deemed and taken to
endure only until the night of Saturday of the week on any day
of which it shall have been stipulated that the service shall
commence; and contracts for executing any particular piece
of work specified in the contract which shall expire so soon as
the work is finished, and when the work is not finished within
a reasonable time, may be put an end to by the master, after
the lapse of a period of time reasonably sufficient for finishing
such work. (1)

No oral contract to be binding for more than one year, and not
   valid unless the time to be entered upon shall be stipulated.

3. No oral contract of service shall be valid or binding for
any longer term than one year from the period fixed for the

(1) Where a compositor, under an engagement by which he was paid at a
rate calculated per 1000 ens and entitled to a week's notice, sued his employer
under sect. 14 of Act 18 of 1873 for withholding wages in lieu of notice, and
no exception to the jurisdiction was taken:
Held, that he was a servant in terms of the Masters and Servants Act:
Held, also, that on appeal to the Supreme Court the objection that the
magistrate had no jurisdiction under Act No. 18, 1873, inasmuch as the Act
only contemplated the withholding of wages already earned, could not be
raised, as it had not been taken in the court below. *Baker* v. *Dormer,*
1 Juta, 253.

Act 15—1856. commencement of the service stipulated for by such contract; and no such oral contract shall be valid or binding in any case, unless it be stipulated in such contract that the service, thereby stipulated for, shall be entered upon by the servant within one month from the date of the contract.

4. [Repealed by § 1 of Act 18, 1873.]

No contract to be valid or binding for a longer period than five years.

5. No such contract so entered into before a magistrate or other proper officer, shall be valid or binding for a longer period than five years from the date thereof, if entered into within this colony; and no such contract shall endure longer than five years from the day of the commencement of the service, when such contract shall be entered into elsewhere than in this colony.

Form of contract of service.

6. All contracts of service entered into before a magistrate or other proper officer, within the limits of this colony, shall be drawn up as nearly as possible in the following terms:

Be it remembered,— that on this ——— day of ——— in the year of our Lord ———, A. B., of ———, and C. D., of ———, appeared before me, E. F. (resident magistrate, or officer specially appointed by the Governor to attest contracts of service for the district, as the case may be, with his usual description), and in my presence, signed their names (or made their marks, as the case may be) to the following contract of service: The said A. B. agrees to hire the service of the said C. D., and the said C. D. agrees to render to the said A. B. his service at all fair and reasonable times, and in the capacity of ——— for ——— commencing on the —— day of ——— instant, and terminating on the ——— day of —— in the year ———. And it is further agreed that the said A. B. shall pay to the said C. D., as such servant as aforesaid, wages after the rate of —— by the day (week, month, or year, as the case may be), and that such wages shall be paid on the ———— day of each week (or Act 15—1856. month, as the case may be).

(Here add any special agreement compatible with the law, and not adverted to in this form.)

(Signed)   A. B.

C. D.

The preceding agreement was signed by the abovenamed parties, in my presence, on the day and year above written, voluntarily, the same being, as far as I am able to judge, understood by them respectively.

(Signed)   E. F.,

Resident Magistrate (or officer specially appointed by the Governor to attest contracts of service for the district).

In the absence of special agreement, one month's notice is required before a contract shall be deemed to have expired.

7. No contract of service for a month or any longer period shall be deemed and taken to have expired until at least one month's notice, calculated from, and inclusive of, the day of giving such notice, shall have been given by either of the parties to the other party, unless it shall have been expressly stipulated that no such notice shall be necessary; and when the service shall be a weekly one, a week's notice shall be necessary : Provided that nothing herein contained shall be construed so as to enable any party to any contract of service to determine the same without the consent of the other party, before the expiration of the term of service originally agreed upon. (1)

(1) Where the parties stand in the relation of master and servant, the mere fact that insufficient notice of discharge has been given does not confer on the servant the right of bringing an action against the master for damages for wrongful dismissal, unless such notice has been acted upon, or unless the period fixed by the notice has actually expired.

If, before the expiration of the notice of discharge, a servant grossly misconducts himself in the service and is dismissed, the master may avail himself of such misconduct as a defence to an action brought against him for wages accruing after such misconduct and dismissal, or to an action for damages sustained by the servant by reason of not being employed after such misconduct. *Nixon v. Blaine & Co.,* Buch, 1879, p. 217 ; *Kenrick v. Central D. M. Co., Ld.,* 3 High Court 414 ; *Douglas v. L. & S. A. Exp. Co.,* 4 High Court 275 ; *Donaldson v. Webber,* 4 High Court 403 ; *Hunt v. E. P. Boating Co.,* 3 E. D. C. 12.

How such notice may be waived.

8. When any such notice as is hereinbefore mentioned shall have been given by either of the parties to the other, and the master shall suffer the servant to remain, or the servant shall remain in his service after the day on which according to the notice given the contract of service should expire, such notice shall be deemed and taken to have been withdrawn and passed from, and the contract of service shall continue to endure as long, and in like manner, as if no such notice had been given unless it shall have been otherwise expressly and specially agreed between the parties.

Servants hired to reside on the premises to be supplied with food and lodging, unless otherwise agreed upon.

9. In all contracts, whether oral or written, by which it is stipulated that the servant shall reside on the premises of his master, and wherein it shall not be expressly provided that the master, is not to supply food and lodging, the master shall be deemed and taken to have engaged to provide such servant, and such of his family (if any) as shall have been included in the contract, in manner hereinafter mentioned, in section twelve of this chapter, with lodging and sufficient food of good and wholesome quality, during the continuance of the contract.

Where a servant on a monthly hiring wilfully deserts his service without notice during the month :
Held, that he was not entitled to claim any wages for the service rendered during that month up to the day of his desertion. *Bassaramadoo v. Morris*, 6 Juta 28.

Where a servant, after his discharge from his master's employment, made an admission with reference to a transaction performed by him by his master's orders during his engagement: *Held*, that the statement so made was not admissible in evidence against the plaintiff, the former master.— *Wood v. Dersley*, 2 E. D. C. 200.

In estimating the amount of damages to be awarded where a servant has been improperly dismissed before the termination of his time of service, the Court will take into consideration any employment which may have been obtained by the servant after dismissal and before the time fixed for the expiration of the contract. *Denny v. S. A. Loan, Mortgage, and Mercantile Agency*, 3 E. D. C. 47.

When rate of wages not specified, the magistrate to fix such rate by custom.

10. In case of any action for non-payment of wages, due and payable by virtue of any contract of service, being brought before any magistrate, or other competent court by any servant, and when the rate of wages at which such contract was made shall not be proved to the satisfaction of such magistrate or court, such magistrate or court is hereby required to fix the rate of wages at that usually paid in the district or place in which the service for which the wages are claimed was performed, reference being had to the skill and ability of the servant, and to give decree accordingly.

Provision in case of sickness.

11. When any servant shall, in consequence of any sickness or accident, which shall not have been occasioned by his own fault, be rendered incapable of performing his master's service, he shall, in the absence of any special provision in the contract to the contrary, be entitled to receive his full wages during the first month of such incapacity, and every other benefit, privilege, or advantage, whether for himself or his family, stipulated for in the contract of service during the whole period of such incapacity, unless the stipulated term of service shall sooner expire, or unless the period of such incapacity shall extend to a longer period than two months; in which latter case the master shall be entitled, if he shall so think fit, at the expiration of such two months, or at any time afterwards during which such incapacity shall uninterruptedly continue, to treat and consider the contract of service as rescinded and determined, to all intents and purposes whatsoever, he, the said master, being however bound, before being so entitled to consider the said contract as determined, to make good all stipulations therein mentioned and agreed upon, up to and for the day on which he shall declare his intention to treat and consider the said contract as rescinded, with, however, the limitation as to wages, hereinbefore provided : Provided, however, that if the master shall not think fit, at or after the expiration of such two months as aforesaid, to treat the con-

Act 15—1856. tract of service as determined and rescinded, but shall permit the servant to remain in his service, such servant shall not be entitled to claim any portion of the wages beyond wages for the first month as aforesaid, or any other benefit or advantage stipulated for in the contract of service (save and except such food and lodging for himself and family as by the contract of service the master had engaged, or shall be deemed and taken to have engaged, to provide him with), for any period subsequent to such two months during which such incapacity as aforesaid shall continue : And provided, always, that no servant hired by any contract expressly to perform service in any trade or handicraft, shall be entitled to receive the wages, or any other benefit or advantage stipulated in the contract of service, for any part of the time during which he shall have been rendered incapable of performing his master's work by any such sickness or accident as aforesaid, save and except such food and lodging for himself or family as by the contract of service his master has engaged to provide him with, such food and lodging to be provided during such incapacity as aforesaid, unless the contract of service shall sooner expire, or unless such incapacity shall extend to a period longer than one month, in which latter case the master shall be entitled, if he shall so think fit, under the same powers and conditions in every respect as in this section before set forth, to treat and consider such last-mentioned contract of service as absolutely, and, to all intents and purposes, determined and rescinded.

Contracts for the services of husband, wife, and children how to be entered into.

12. All contracts of service stipulating for the services of the wife of any servant, together with those of her husband, shall be made or executed by her in like manner as the same shall be made and executed by her said husband : And it shall be lawful for the father, or, in the event of his death or absence, then for the mother, of any child under the age of sixteen years, to contract for the service of such child together with his own, in like manner as such person may contract for his own services; and when such contract shall be in writing, the name and age of every such child shall be clearly set forth

and specified in the contract: Provided always, that nothing herein contained shall give to the master of any such parent any claim on the services of any such child beyond the period for which the parent shall be engaged, nor beyond the period when such child shall attain the age of sixteen; nor to the services of any other child of the contracting parent, whether under colour of such last-mentioned child having been fed or clothed by the master, or having been born while the parent of such child was in the said master's service, or under any other pretence whatsoever.

One month after the death of the husband, contract to be null and void with regard to the services of the wife and children.

13. On the death of any person being at the time, together with his wife and any child, under contract as aforesaid, the contract shall become null and void, with respect to such wife and children, at the expiration of one month after the death of such person.

Wife and children of the servant not to reside on the premises of the master, unless stipulated in the contract, nor the master to claim their services by reason merely of their residence on the premises.

14. It shall not be lawful for any person entering into any contract of service by which it is stipulated that the servant shall himself reside on the premises of the master, to keep his wife and children on the premises of his master, unless when the master shall have also stipulated in such contract that this shall and may be done; Provided that, when the master shall have so stipulated, it shall not be lawful for him to claim the services of any such wife or child by reason merely of their residence on his premises.

An agricultural labourer or herdsman to remain in his master's service during public commotion or invasion of the colony, or if called out for burgher service the master to provide for his family.

15. When, in times of public commotion or invasion of the colony, the Governor shall deem it expedient to call out for

Act 15—1856. service any portion of the burgher force of any division of the colony, under the Act No. 16 of 1855, (1) every person under contract of service under this Act, as an agricultural labourer or herdsman, for any period not less than one month, to any master residing in such division, shall, if the period of service contracted for should expire during the persistence of such commotion or invasion, notwithstanding such expiration, be bound to continue in the service of his employer, on the terms of the contract under which he had been serving, until the cessation of such commotion or invasion, and until the services of the burghers of such division shall be dispensed with for the occasion : Provided that, if any such servant shall at any time be called out for burgher service under the said Act No. 16, 1855, (1) the master of such servant shall, during the absence of such servant on such duty, be bound to permit the family and property of such servant to remain upon his premises, and to provide for the same, in the same manner as he would have been bound to do by the contract of service, if such servant had not proceeded to the performance of such duty.

CHAPTER III.

ON THE APPRENTICESHIP OF CHILDREN (2).

Contracts to be in writing.

1. No contract of apprenticeship shall be valid unless, at the time of its being entered into, it shall have been reduced into writing, and signed with the name, or, in case of illiterate persons, with the mark, of the master and parent, (3) or guardian, as the case may be, of the apprentice, and also of the apprentice if of the full age of sixteen years.

(1) Act 16 of 1855 is repealed by Act 7 of 1878 (Defence).
(2) Any child convicted of any offence may be bound to some useful calling or occupation until such child shall attain the age of 16 years. Act 7, 1879 (Reformatory Institutions), § 4. See also Act 8, 1889, *infra.*
(3) The conviction of a minor for neglect of duty under a contract of service entered into by him without the consent of his parent, quashed. —Buch, 1879, p. 288.

A. 15—1856.

Children under 16 to be apprenticed to agricultural labour only till that age.

2. No contract of apprenticeship by which any child under sixteen years, if a female, and eighteen years if a male, may be apprenticed as an agricultural or domestic servant, shall be valid for any longer period than until such child shall have attained the full age of sixteen years, if a female, and eighteen years, if a male.

Children, not destitute, above 10 and under 16 years, may be apprenticed till 21.

3. Children not being in a state of destitution, above the age of ten, and under the age of sixteen years, may be apprenticed by their fathers, (1) or, in the case of fatherless children, by their mothers, or, in case of orphans, having guardians, by their guardians, until they shall have attained their twenty-first year, or for any shorter period, and due provision for the maintenance, clothing, and instruction of every such apprentice shall be made in the contract of apprenticeship: Provided always, that every contract of apprenticeship, whereby any child under the age of ten years, not being in a state of destitution, shall

(1) In the Supreme Court on the 9th of August, 1889, the Chief Justice said that as judge of the week a case had been brought before him for review. It was a case where a lad, Peter Kruger, was charged with absenting himself from his master's service without proper cause or authority. The lad was found guilty, and sentenced to receive fifteen cuts with a cane. It appeared that the lad was only fifteen years of age, and that no proper contract of apprenticeship had been executed with the master. There seemed, however, to have been a verbal contract between the father of the child, Peter Kruger, and the master. The question was whether under such a contract the child could be punished for the offence of desertion. He (the Chief Justice) had looked over the Masters and Servants Act, and he found there were only two ways in which a minor could be contracted for, either by contract of apprenticeship or by engaging the services of the child, together with the services of one of the parents. If one of the parents served the same master with the child, then the contract was valid. But unless this was done there would have to be a regular contract of apprenticeship. In the present case there was no such thing. The contract was made without either of the parents serving the same master at the same time as the lad. There appeared to him (the Chief Justice) to be no legal contract, and so the lad could not be punished for desertion. The sentence of the magistrate was accordingly quashed.

Act 15—1856. be apprenticed, or attempted so to be, shall be null and void to all intents and purposes whatsoever; save and except a contract of apprenticeship executed by the parent or guardian, and the master, in the presence of a resident magistrate and attested by such magistrate to be a contract which appears to him to be for the benefit of the child.

Persons of 16 years and upwards may, by their own consent, be apprenticed for five years.

4. (1) Any minor of the full age of sixteen years or upwards may, by his own consent, be apprenticed for any term not exceeding five years to any trade, in the practice of which any peculiar art or skill is required, but not otherwise : Provided always, that in the case of such minor or minors being females, they may, with such consent, be apprenticed to domestic service for any such period as last aforesaid.

Resident magistrate to be the guardian, ex officio, of minors who have no parents or guardians.

5. (2) The resident magistrates of the colony shall be, *ex officio* the guardians, within their respective districts, of all such minors as in the last preceding section mentioned, which minors have no parents or guardians within the colony, or none discoverable, and such resident magistrates may lawfully indenture such minors.

Destitute children, how to be treated in the first instance.

6. When any parent or parents shall abandon or desert, or by death shall leave, in a state of destitution any child under

(1) Where an apprentice, who had been duly articled before a Resident Magistrate for a term of five years, during that period absented himself from his master's service, and then agreed with the master that, instead of being punished for such absence by the magistrate, he would work out the time he had been absent after the expiration of the term of apprenticeship, but at the end of the five years repudiated the agreement, the master cannot withhold the wages earned by the apprentice under his articles, on the ground that he had not carried out the agreement to work out the lost time.

Costs follow the result, where an appeal is based upon a question of law which is not ambiguous. *Njoli* v. *Stewart,* 1 E. D. C. 147.

(2) A magistrate has no power to sentence a prisoner, on his trial for theft to be indentured as an apprentice. *R.* v. *Jan & Booy,* Buch, 1874, p. 63.

the age of sixteen years, the person with whom such child shall have been so left, or by whom such child shall be found in such state of destitution, shall, with all convenient speed, give notice thereof to the nearest field-cornet, or directly to the magistrate, in order that means may be taken for providing for the maintenance and education of such child, by apprenticeship, in manner hereinafter mentioned ; and if any person shall be duly convicted by any magistrate or other competent court of detaining in his possession or employment any such destitute child as aforesaid for a longer period than one month without giving such notice, every such person shall forfeit and pay, at a rate not exceeding twenty, nor less than five shillings for each month that such child shall have been detained ; and every such sum so forfeited shall be paid into the public treasury ; and all reasonable expense incurred in giving such notice, and for the maintenance of such child until removed by the proper authority, shall be paid from the said treasury.

Destitute children how to be apprenticed.

7. The field-cornet or resident magistrate shall, upon receiving such notice as aforesaid, cause the child to be removed to the residence of such magistrate, and the said magistrate shall, unless when it shall be made to appear to him that the child is actually not in a state of destitution, or is able to earn his own livelihood (in either of which events he shall decline to act in the case), cause such child to be lodged and provided for at the public cost, until he shall have sufficiently ascertained by inquiry, which he is hereby required to cause to be made, whether such child have any relative, fit, proper, and willing to maintain and take care of him, and if he shall discover any such relative or relatives, he shall apprentice such child, either to the sole relative, or to that one among the several relatives of whom it shall appear most for the interest of such child to become the apprentice ; and if no such fit and proper relative be found, he shall apprentice him, as soon as a suitable opportunity can be found, to some fit and proper person, until he shall have attained his eighteenth year, or in the case of females, until their sixteenth year, or for any shorter period that may be deemed advisable. And every

Act 15—1856. such magistrate shall give public notice in the *Government Gazette* of the name of every such apprentice and of the person to whom he shall have been apprenticed.

Maintenance and wages to be stipulated for on behalf of such destitute children when apprenticed.

8. Due provision for the maintenance, clothing, and instruction of every destitute child so apprenticed shall be made in every such contract of apprenticeship, and suitable wages shall also be therein stipulated for, whenever such magistrate or other proper officer shall deem that the child's service in any part thereof will be worth wages; and in apprenticing every such child, either to a relative or stranger, it shall be the duty of such magistrate or officer to make the best terms he can for such child.

Form of contract in apprenticing destitute children.

9. All such contracts for the apprenticeship of destitute children as aforesaid shall be drawn up as near as possible in the following terms:—

District of ———.

This contract of apprenticeship of A. B. (here insert the designation of A. B. as accurately as possible), a destitute child, witnesseth that C. D. (here describe C. D. as the resident magistrate, or as the officer specially appointed by the Governor to attest such contracts of apprenticeship for the district, as the case may be), pursuant to the Act No.—in that case made and provided, does by these presents apprentice the said A. B., aged years or thereabouts, to E. F. (here insert the designation of E. F. as accurately as possible), with him to dwell and serve as an apprentice until (or for, as the case may be —here insert the age at which the apprenticeship is to determine, or the term for which it is to endure), during all which time the said apprentice shall faithfully and honestly serve and obey his master; and the said E. F., for himself, his heirs, and executors, does hereby covenant and agree with the said C. D., for and on behalf of the said A. B., that he, the said E. F., shall teach and instruct, or cause to be taught and instructed, the said A. B. in the (here insert the particular trade or occupation), in the best manner that he can, during the said term, and shall also duly provide, or cause due provision to be made, for the education and religious instruction of the said A. B. to the best of his ability, and shall, during the said term, provide the said apprentice with suitable and sufficient food, washing, lodging, and all other things necessary and fit for such apprentice, and shall also pay, as wages, to the said apprentice, the sum of (here insert the terms at which the wages stipulated are to be payable); and also, the said E. F. shall not assign or transfer the said apprentice to any other person during the said term, without the consent, in writing, first had and obtained, of the magistrate or other proper officer having power and authority to give such consent.

In witness whereof, we, the said C. D. and E. F., have set our hands at —— on this the —— day of —— 18—
(Here insert the signatures or marks of the parties)

In presence of (here shall be inserted the signatures of at least two witnesses, who have witnessed the execution of the contract).

Covenants in such contracts to endure to successor in office of the magistrate in whose favour they are made.

10. In case the magistrate or other proper officer by whom the contract for the apprenticeship of any such destitute child as aforesaid shall have been entered into as aforesaid shall, by death or otherwise, cease to act as such magistrate or officer, then, and in that case, all the provisions and covenants in such contract of apprenticeship contained shall endure in favour of the successor of such magistrate or officer, duly appointed, and such successor shall and may sue upon and take all other benefit and advantage whatsoever of such provisions and covenants, in like manner as if such successor had been himself the person by whom such contract as aforesaid was originally made.

C

Such contracts of apprenticeship shall be in three parts,—one to be given to the master, one to the apprentice, and the third to be filed in the office of the magistrate.

11. Every such last-mentioned contract of apprenticeship shall be made and signed as aforesaid in three parts, one of which parts shall be given to the master, and one to the apprentice, and the third shall be filed and registered in the office of the magistrate by whom it is attested; or, where it shall have been attested by any other officer specially appointed as aforesaid, an entry of it shall be made in a book to be kept by him for that purpose, and the said third part shall be transmitted by him to the magistrate of the district in which the master by whom such contract has been made usually resides, to be filed and registered in his office.

Apprentice not to be assigned without consent of magistrate, or when apprentice shall be sixteen years, without his own consent.

12. No master shall or may assign or transfer any apprentice, having been apprenticed as aforesaid by any magistrate or other proper officer as aforesaid, to any other person, without the consent, in writing, first had and obtained, of the magistrate or other proper officer of the district in which such master resides; and in case such apprentice shall be of the age of sixteen years, or upwards, without the consent of such apprentice himself.

CHAPTER IV.

RESPECTING THE EFFECTS OF THE DEATH, INSOLVENCY, AND CHANGE OF RESIDENCE OF THE MASTER; AND OTHER CIRCUMSTANCES DISSOLVING CONTRACTS OF SERVICE WITHOUT NOTICE.

Effect of death or insolvency of master upon the contract of service.

1. In the event of the death or insolvency (1) of the master, the contract of service shall, except as hereafter excepted, cease and determine after one month from the date of such

(1) *Clark* v. *Denny,* 4 E. D. C. 300.

death or insolvency, in case the stipulated term of service shall Act 15—1856.
not sooner expire ; and up to the period of such determination of
such contract, such servant shall be entitled to claim his full
wages and every other remuneration specified in such contract,
and shall be bound, if required, to perform his service for
the person legally representing the deceased or insolvent
master.

Effect of death or insolvency of master upon the contract of apprenticeship.

2. In the event of the death or insolvency of the master
of any apprentice, or in the event of the apprentice being
prevented, in the manner hereinafter in the sixth section of this
chapter particularly mentioned, from performing his service
or fulfilling his engagement at the place where the same ought
to be performed or fulfilled, such death, insolvency or pre-
vention shall be a complete discharge of the contract of
apprenticeship, and if any sum shall have been really and
bonâ fide paid by or on behalf of such apprentice as aforesaid,
it shall be lawful for any magistrate having jurisdiction, or
other competent court, upon proof of such payment, to order,
in a summary manner, any sum which to the said magistrate
or court shall seem reasonable to be paid to or for the use of
such apprentice as aforesaid, by any such master as aforesaid,
or his legal representative ; regard being had, however, in
estimating such sum, to the amount of the sum originally paid
by or on behalf of such apprentice, and to the time during which,
such apprentice continued in the service of such master as
aforesaid ; Provided always, that every such apprentice shall
be entitled to his full wages, or other remuneration, which
may have become due previous to such dissolution of the
contract of apprenticeship.

Effect of death or insolvency of master where apprentice is under or of the age of 16.

3. In the event of the death or insolvency of the master
of any child, who having been in a state of destitution, shall
have been apprenticed by a magistrate or other proper officer
in the manner hereinbefore set forth, it shall be the duty of

Act 15—1856. such magistrate or other proper officer, in case such apprentice shall, at the time of the death or insolvency of his former master, be under the age of sixteen years, and unable to support himself, to retake the charge and care of such child; and if it shall be deemed expedient, to apprentice again the said child for any term within the limits prescribed by this bill for the duration of apprenticeship to such fit and proper person as such magistrate or other proper officer and such child, if of the age of sixteen years or upwards, shall mutually approve of and agree upon; Provided that when such child has not attained the said age of sixteen years, his consent shall not be necessary in any case.

Widow of deceased master may adopt the contract of service.

4. The wife of the deceased master of every servant or apprentice, hired or contracted to perform service as a domestic or agricultural servant, is entitled, if she shall so think fit, to claim the service of such servant or apprentice during the full period of the stipulated term of service, provided she shall consent to perform, and shall perform, all the stipulations of the contract in favour of the servant or apprentice which the master was bound to perform.

On death of servant or apprentice, wages to be paid up to period of death.

5. In the event of a servant or apprentice dying during the currency of the stipulated term of service, his heirs, executors, or other legal representatives, are entitled to claim from the master the full wages and other remuneration due to such servant or apprentice for the period which he had served previously to his death, and no more.

Effect of change of residence of master upon the contract of service or apprenticeship.

6. No servant or apprentice (save as hereafter provided as to persons apprenticed as destitute children), hired or contracted to perform service at the residence of, or at any particular place of trade or business, occupied by his master, is, in the event of his master's removing his residence, or place

of trade or business, out of the town, or (where such place Act 15—1856. is not in any town) from the place in which by the contract such servant or apprentice was bound to perform his service, to any greater distance than two miles from such town or place where, by the stipulations of the contract, such servant or apprentice is not bound to reside in the house or on the premises of his master, or out of the district of such town or place where such servant or apprentice is bound to reside in the house or on the premises of his master,—bound to perform his service at the place to which his master shall have removed his residence or place of trade or business, without the consent of such servant, or of the parents or guardians of such apprentice;—but such consent shall in all cases be deemed and taken to have been given whenever it shall be proved that such servant, or apprentice, being one not bound to reside in the house or on the premises of his master, has performed, or in the case of an apprentice, been knowingly permitted and allowed by his parent or guardian to perform, at the new residence or place of trade or business of his master, any service to his master of any kind which he was bound by the contract to perform,—or being one bound to reside in his master's house or premises, has gone to and remained, and in the case of an apprentice, been permitted and allowed by his parent or guardian to go to and remain in such house or on such premises, for one week after his master's removal thereto.

The master of an apprentice, who shall have been a destitute child, may remove such apprentice, with permission of magistrate.

7. The master of any apprentice who has been apprenticed to him in manner hereinbefore provided as a destitute child is entitled, without limitation or restraint, to remove such apprentice to and to exact the performance of the service stipulated in the contract wherever such master may have removed his residence or place of trade or business within this colony, upon giving notice of his intention so to do before his departure to the magistrate of the district which he is going to leave, and the magistrate, upon receiving such notice, shall

Act 15—1856. endorse the same on the third part of the contract of apprenticeship registered and filed by him; and on such removal taking place, forthwith transmit such third part to the magistrate of the district to which such an apprentice shall be removed, to be by him duly registered and filed in manner hereinbefore provided.

Certain servants and apprentices bound to make certain journeys, if required.

8. No servant or apprentice, hired or contracted to perform domestic service, may lawfully refuse to accompany his master, or any of his family, by desire of his master, on any journey within this colony, or in the course of such journey to perform every such service as, by reason of his contract of service or apprenticeship, he would be bound to perform in his master's house or on his premises; and no servant or apprentice may lawfully refuse to go on any journey within this colony on which his master shall order him to go, or in charge of, or to drive, herd, tend, or take care of any carriage, horse, or any kind of cattle, the property or in the lawful possession of or under the lawful control of his master, which such servant or apprentice would, by reason of his contract of service or apprenticeship, be bound to ride, drive, herd, tend or take care of, or charge of, at his master's residence or on his premises : Provided always, that there shall be reasonable ground for believing that such journey may and will be performed before the expiration of the stipulated term of the service of such servant or apprentice; and that such master shall be bound to provide such servant or apprentice with food and every other thing which may be necessary and proper to enable such servant or apprentice to perform such journey, and to return to the residence or premises of his master before the expiration of the term of service.

No servant or apprentice shall be bound to accompany his master or go out of the colony without special agreement or consent.

9. No servant or apprentice shall be bound to accompany his master or to go out of this colony, without the special

agreement or consent of such servant, or of the parent or guardian of such apprentice, or when such apprentice is of the full age of sixteen years, without, also, the consent of such apprentice.

Act 15—1856

Where servant not bound to accompany his master to new residence, contract dissolved by master's removal.

10. When any servant not being bound or obliged to accompany his master, or go to any place to which the master shall remove his residence or place of trade or business, or to which the master shall order such servant to go, shall decline or refuse so to do, the contract of service shall, from the date on which the servant shall be prevented from performing his stipulated service at the place where the same was to have been performed, stand dissolved, and such servant shall be entitled to claim from the master such wages or other remuneration, at the rate specified in the contract of service, as shall have been earned up to the time of the refusal before mentioned, together with wages and remuneration after the rate aforesaid for the period of one month additional, or until the expiration of the contract of service, in case it shall expire within one month from the time of such refusal: Provided always, that when notice of his intention to remove as aforesaid, or to send such servant as aforesaid, shall have been given by such master, such additional wages and remuneration shall not in any case be due or payable for any period longer than one month from the date of such notice.

Any special agreement touching change of residence to be good.

11. Nothing herein contained shall annul or affect any special agreement or stipulation, made in any contract of service or apprenticeship, whereby the servant or apprentice shall be bound to accompany his master, or to go to any place, to which the master shall remove his residence or place of trade or business, or order such servant or apprentice to go and there perform the service stipulated in such contract.

Effect of marriage of female servant or apprentice, as to right of husband.

12. When any female servant or apprentice shall be lawfully married during the currency of her stipulated term of service, her husband may at any time subsequent to such marriage dissolve the contract of service or apprenticeship, and remove his wife from her master's service, if he shall think fit so to do, and shall be entitled to claim the wages and other remuneration which may have become due to her, for services previously to such removal, but shall be liable to her master for all damage which her master may sustain by such removal. But such damages shall in no case exceed the amount of the wages which she would have earned between the time of her marriage, and the time of the expiration of her service, had she continued in such service until such expiration.

Effect of marriage or pregnancy of female servant or apprentice, as to the rights of master.

13. The master of any female servant or apprentice, who during the currency of her stipulated term of service, shall marry or enter into any state which in this colony is or shall be reputed to be the marriage state, shall, where such servant or apprentice is, by her contract of service or apprenticeship, bound to reside or to perform domestic service in the house or on the premises of her master, be entitled, at any time subsequent to such marriage or reputed marriage, to dissolve such contract and dismiss such servant or apprentice, and when such servant or apprentice is not by such contract bound to reside or to perform domestic service, in the house or the premises of her master, he shall be entitled to dissolve such contract, and dismiss such servant or apprentice from his service, whenever she shall, by reason of her pregnancy or delivery of a child, become disabled from performing the service which, by such contract she is bound to perform; but any such servant or apprentice so dismissed on account of her marriage, or entering into a state so reputed as aforesaid to be the marriage state, or of pregnancy or delivery of child, shall be entitled to claim from her master the wages and every other

remuneration which shall have become due to her for her Act 15—1856.
services previously to the date of such dismissal; and the
master, before being entitled to dismiss such servant or apprentice, shall be bound to pay and satisfy the same.

CHAPTER V.

Of the Jurisdiction of the Resident Magistrates in cases between Masters and Servants and Apprentices.

Jurisdiction of resident magistrates in cases between masters and their servants and apprentices.

1. The resident magistrates within the colony have jurisdiction in all cases arising in their respective districts between
masters and their servants and apprentices, and with reference
to their relative rights and duties, or to any matter or thing,
or offence, as to which provision is made by this bill.

Resident magistrates have jurisdiction over all persons within their respective districts.

2. Every resident magistrate has jurisdiction in any such
case as aforesaid, brought before him against any person being
at the time within his district, whether the grounds of such
case arose within the district or not, or whether the person
against whom the case is brought has his usual residence or
place of abode in that district or not; but the magistrate
shall, whenever it shall appear to him that any such case can
be more conveniently tried or determined by the resident
magistrate of any other district, dismiss such case, and, in the
event of his doing so, when the servant or apprentice is
accused of desertion, and when he shall have probable cause
shown to him, by oath or affidavit, of any credible person, for
believing this to be the fact, such magistrate may, if he think
fit, issue a warrant for the conveyance, under sure custody, of
such servant or apprentice to the town or place where the
court of such other magistrate is held; Provided the master

Act 15—1856. shall undertake to pay the expense of such conveyance, and the magistrate by whom the cause shall be ultimately tried and decided shall adjudge by which of the parties the said expenses shall be paid.

3. [§§ 3–9 repealed by § 21 of Act 18 of 1873.]

Definition of punishment for servant refusing to resume his service after undergoing imprisonment.

10. If any servant or apprentice, whose contract of service or apprenticeship still subsists, shall, upon being discharged from prison after undergoing imprisonment under this Act, refuse or neglect, upon his master's request, to resume his service under his contract, he shall be liable to be imprisoned with or without hard labour for any period not exceeding one month, and so on for successive periods, not any of them exceeding one month, until he shall consent to resume, and shall resume, his service under his contract; and every such period of imprisonment, or so much thereof as the convicting magistrate shall adjudge, may be with solitary confinement with or without spare diet, or with spare diet with or without solitary confinement: Provided, however, that no servant or apprentice shall, under this Act be imprisoned continuously, and without any intermediate resumption of service, under his contract, for longer than six months in all.

Period of imprisonment of servant to be added to the term of service stipulated in the contract.

11. When any period of imprisonment shall be undergone by any servant or apprentice for any offence under this Act, a like period shall be added to the term of service stipulated for in the contract of service or apprenticeship, as it subsisted when such imprisonment was commenced, so that such servant or apprentice shall be obliged to serve a further period equal to the period of his imprisonment, in addition to the term of service originally stipulated.

Period during which any servant shall have absented himself *from the service of his master to be added to the term of service originally stipulated.*

12. (1) When the offence of which any servant or apprentice shall be convicted under this Act, shall be the offence of absenting himself from, or of departing from, the service of his master, then the period of his absence shall be added to the term of service originally stipulated, in like manner as in the last preceding section directed in regard to the period of imprisonment therein mentioned; and it shall be the duty of the magistrate convicting such servant or apprentice, to ascertain, at the trial, the period of absence, and to certify the same by some writing under his hand, to be delivered to the master, and the period mentioned in such writing shall, by all courts and in all places, be deemed to be added to the original term of service.

Compensation by servant for loss of or damage to property of master.

13. As often as any property of the master shall be lost or damaged by means of any act or omission of his servant or apprentice, which act or omission is by this Act declared to be an offence, it shall be lawful for the magistrate, should he so think fit, and the master shall thereto agree, to ascertain whether such servant or apprentice is able to make compensation for such loss or damage, and if so, to fix the amount of such compensation, and make such order as to the payment thereof, either at once or by instalments out of wages to be yet earned, or otherwise, as shall seem reasonable and just, and in the meantime, and until default made in such payment, or in the payment of such some instalment, to defer passing sentence upon the party offending; but such magistrate shall preserve on record the evidence in the case, and, upon application of the master, and proof given, upon oath, of some such default as aforesaid, shall issue his warrant for the apprehension of such servant or apprentice, and shall pronounce upon him such sentence as, regard being had to the circumstances of the original offence, and to the degree

(1) *Njoli* v. *Stewart,* 1 E. D. C. 147.

in which such servant or apprentice has made, or failed to make, the compensation ordered, shall appear equitable and just. (1)

Cancellation of contract for misconduct of servant.

14. As often as the master of any servant or apprentice, who shall be convicted of any offence under this Act, shall desire the cancellation of the contract of service or apprenticeship, the magistrate, should he so think fit, may order the cancellation of the same, and the same shall be cancelled accordingly; Provided that such cancellation shall not prevent the execution of any sentence which the magistrate may pronounce or may have pronounced upon the offender for his offence.

Cancellation of contract on groundless accusation by the master.

15. As often as the master shall have caused any servant or apprentice to be brought before the magistrate to answer any charge preferred against him by such master, and such master shall fail in obtaining the conviction of such servant or apprentice, then the magistrate should he so think fit, may, at the desire of such servant or apprentice, order the cancellation of the contract of service or apprenticeship, and the same shall be cancelled accordingly.

16. [§§ 16–20 repealed by § 21 of Act 18 of 1873.]

(1) Where upon a trial and conviction for theft of stock the owner of the stock applies for judgment against the prisoner, who was his servant, for the damage suffered, the proceedings should be taken under Act 16 of 1864, § 4, and not under the Masters and Servants Act, No. 15, 1856, section 13.

Where compensation is asked against a prisoner convicted of theft of stock, the value of the property stolen must be proved.—*Queen* v. *Jack,* 2 E. D. C. 388.

A servant convicted for breach of duty whereby his master's property is lost, cannot be sentenced to imprisonment and to pay the value of the property lost.—*Queen* v. *Whitbooy,* 2 E. D. C. 161.

If a servant has goods of his master in his possession, and by a subsequent contract, either by pledge or sale, the property is intended to be passed to the servant, there need not be an actual fresh delivery, per De Villiers C.J. *O'Callaghan's Assignees* v. *Cavanagh,* 2 Juta 122.

Actions by servants to compel delivery of property detained.   Act 15—1856.

21. (1) *The magistrates of this colony have jurisdiction in any civil case instituted by any servant or apprentice, to compel the delivery of any of his cattle, sheep, goats, or other animals, lawfully running or being upon his master's land, and which his master shall, either before or after the expiration of the contract of service or apprenticeship, upon demand made, and without lawful cause, have refused to deliver or permit to be taken away; and in case it shall be made to appear that the master had no reasonable and probable cause for believing that the animals in question were lawfully detained, the magistrate shall, besides giving judgment for the delivery of such animals, and for costs, impose, at the same time, upon the master, a fine not exceeding one pound for every animal so unlawfully detained: Provided, however, that the total amount of the fine so payable shall not exceed the sum of five pounds altogether; such fine to be recoverable in like manner as the said costs, but, when recovered, to be applied as by this Act directed, in regard to fines in criminal cases: Provided that neither the fact that the contract of service or apprenticeship of such servant or apprentice has not yet expired, nor the fact that money is due or alleged to be due by such servant or apprentice to the master, shall be deemed or taken to be, of itself, reasonable and probable cause for such detention: Provided, however, that nothing herein contained shall impair the effect of any express contract of lawful kind, by force of which the master shall claim a right to retain any such animals as aforesaid.*

22. [§§ 22 & 23 repealed by § 21 of Act 18 of 1873.]

Contract may be cancelled if the master has wrongfully assaulted his servant or apprentice.

24. As often as any master shall be convicted of wrongfully and unlawfully assaulting his servant or apprentice, the convicting magistrate may, should he so think fit, and should the servant or apprentice so desire, order the cancellation of the contract of service or apprenticeship, and the same shall be cancelled accordingly.

25. [§§ 25 & 26 repealed by § 21 of Act 18 of 1873.]

(1)   This section is repealed by Act 18 of 1873, but is reprinted in view of the provisions of § 3 Act 14 of 1870 (Cattle Removal); see, however, § 15, Act 18 of 1873, *infra.*

Detaining a child under 16 years of age.

27. If any child under the age of sixteen years shall be wrongfully detained by any person as a servant or inmate, the resident magistrate of the district in which it shall be so detained, shall have jurisdiction to order the restoration of such child to such of its parents as would, under this Act, be entitled to apprentice such child, if then about to be apprenticed : Provided, however, that should it be made to appear, upon the hearing of any such case, that the person complained against originally obtained the said child in a lawful manner, and when an infant under the age of five years, and that the parent claiming the same has so acted in reference to the said child, and to the person bringing it up, as to make it a breach of good faith on the part of such parent to seek to take it away, as he or she now seeks to do, and that from the character of the said parent, the purpose for which he or she appears to desire to obtain possession of the said child, or other circumstances, it will be for the manifest benefit of the said child to remain with the person with whom it is residing, rather than to be delivered to the parent applying, then the magistrate shall refuse to order the delivery of the said child, leaving it to the parent applying for the same to take such other proceedings, if any, as he or she may be advised; and such magistrate may, in the meantime, authorize the person rearing up such child to retain possession thereof.

Attorney-General and the clerks of the peace to act for servants, respondent, in cases of appeal to Supreme or circuit court.

28. In any case between a master and his servant, or apprentice, in which the resident magistrate shall have given judgment in favour of such servant or apprentice, and such master shall appeal from such judgment, or apply to have the same reviewed, it shall be the duty of the Attorney-General, in case such appeal or application shall be brought before the Supreme Court, and of the clerk of the peace for the district in which such judgment was made, in case such appeal or application shall be brought before the circuit court (provided

the said Attorney-General or such clerk of the peace shall be Act 15—1856 called on so to do), to appear for and conduct the case of such servant or apprentice, free of all charge or expense whatever, and the judge of the circuit court is hereby empowered, upon the motion of any such clerk of the peace, to assign counsel to act gratuitously for such servant or apprentice whenever such judge shall be of opinion that it is fit and proper so to do.

CHAPTER VI.

RESPECTING CHARACTERS GIVEN BY MASTERS TO SERVANTS OR APPRENTICES.

No master is bound to give a character of a servant.

1. No master is bound to give a character to any servant or apprentice, who is or has been in his service, or to assign any reason for refusing to give it.

Consequences of knowingly giving a false character.

2. Every master who shall knowingly have given any false character to any servant or apprentice is liable to make compensation for any loss or damages which any third party, who, by reason of such character so given, has been induced to take such servant or apprentice into his service, has sustained by the misconduct of such servant or apprentice in any respect, or with reference to any matter to which such character so given was false.

Penalties for counterfeit certificates of character and false representations.

3. Every person who for the purpose of giving a character to any servant or apprentice, or other person intending to offer himself to be hired as a servant, shall forge or counterfeit and utter any certificate of such servant's or apprentice's character, or shall falsely personate any other person, and as such, either personally or by writing, give any false, forged, or counterfeit character, or certificate of character, of any such servant

Act 15—1856. apprentice, or other person offering or intending to offer to hire himself as a servant; and every person who shall offer to hire as a servant, asserting or pretending that he has served in any service in which he has not actually served, or with a false, forged, or counterfeit certificate of character, or shall in any wise add to or alter, by effacing, or erasing, or inserting any word or date, in any certificate given to him by his present or any former master, or by any other person duly authorized by any such master to give the same, and shall use, or attempt to use, the same, as an inducement to hire him, shall, on conviction thereof, incur and be liable to a fine not exceeding fifty pounds, nor less than ten pounds, or to be imprisoned for any period not exceeding one year, nor less than one month, or to both such fine and imprisonment.

CHAPTER VII.

Respecting the Constraints of Masters, Servants, and Apprentices.

Definition and punishment of unlawful interference with servants or apprentices, in order to prevent them from entering into or completing contract of service or apprenticeship.

1. Any person who shall by violence to the person or property, or by threats or intimidation, or by molesting, or in any way obstructing another, force or endeavour to force any servant or apprentice to depart from his service or work, or to return his work to his master before the same shall be finished, or to prevent or endeavour to prevent any servant or other person, not being hired or employed, from hiring himself to, or accepting service or work from any person, or force or induce, or endeavour to force or induce, any such servant or apprentice, or other such person, to belong to any club or association, or to contribute to any common fund, or shall use or employ violence to the property of another, or threats or intimidation, or shall molest or in any way obstruct another on account of his not belonging to any particular club or association, or not having contributed, or having refused to contribute, to any common

fund, or to pay any fine or penalty, or on account of his not Act 15—1856.
having complied, or of his refusing to comply, with any rules,
orders, resolutions, and regulations, made to obtain an advance
or to reduce the rate of wages, or to lessen or alter the hours
of working, or to decrease or alter the quantity of work, or to
regulate the mode of carrying on any manufacture, trade,
business, work, or labour, or the management thereof; or who,
by any such violence, threats, intimidation, molestation, or
obstruction, shall force, or endeavour to force, any manufacturer,
or person carrying on any trade, business, work, or labour, or
engaged in agriculture, to make any alteration in his mode of
regulating, managing, conducting, or carrying on the same, or
to increase or limit the number of his apprentices or servants,
shall on conviction thereof before any resident magistrate, or
other competent court, be imprisoned with or without hard
labour, for any period not exceeding three months.

Definition and protection of lawful acts and associations.

2. Provided always that nothing herein contained shall
extend to subject to punishment any persons who shall meet
together for the sole purpose of consulting upon and deter-
mining the rate of wages or prices which the persons present
at that meeting, or any of them respectively, shall require or
demand for his or their service or work, or shall pay his or their
servants or apprentices for their service or work, or who shall
enter into any agreement, verbal or written, among themselves,
for the purpose of fixing the rate of wages or prices, which
rate of wages or prices the persons entering into such agreement, or any of them, shall require or demand for his or their
service or work, or pay to his or their servants or apprentices
for their service or work, or of fixing the number of hours of
work which he or they will work, or will require his or their
servants or apprentices to work in any manufacture, trade,
business, labour, or agriculture, and that no such persons so
meeting together, or entering into any such agreement as
aforesaid, shall be liable to any penalty or prosecution for so
doing.

No. 18—1873.] (1)   AN ACT   [June 26, 1873.

To Amend Act No. 15, 1856, intituled "An Act to amend the Laws regulating the relative Rights and Duties of Masters, Servants, and Apprentices."

Preamble.

Whereas it is expedient to amend the Act No. 15 of 1856, intituled "An Act to amend the Laws regulating the relative Rights and Duties of ·Masters, Servants, and Apprentices: " Be it therefore enacted by the Governor of the Cape of Good Hope, with the advice and consent of the Legislative Council and House of Assembly thereof, as follows :

Fourth section of chapter 2 of Act 15 of 1856 repealed.—Written contract of service not valid for more than one year except on certain conditions.

1. (1) The fourth section of chapter 2 of Act No. 15 of 1856, intituled " An Act to amend the Laws regulating the relative Rights and Duties of Masters, Servants, and Apprentices," shall be and the same is hereby repealed ; and from and after the promulgation of this Act no written contract of service entered into in this Colony shall be valid or binding for a longer period than one year from the date thereof, nor shall any contract for service in writing be valid or binding in any case on any servant, unless the service so contracted for shall be stipulated to commence within the period of one month from the date of the contract, except the contract be signed with the name, or, in case of illiterate persons, with the mark, of the contracting parties, in the presence of a magistrate, or other proper officer, described in the second section of Act No. 15 of 1856, who shall satisfy himself by inquiry of the servant or apprentice that the contract was entered into

(1) A prisoner cannot be convicted of a contravention of the Masters and Servants Law Amendment Act, 1873, alleged to have been committed beyond the jurisdiction of the Supreme Court of this colony. *Queen* v. *Baartman Jakhals,* 3 E. D. C. 118.

by the parties voluntarily, and with a clear understanding of Act 18—1873. its meaning and effect, and shall then, and not till then, subscribe such written contract in attestation of that fact.

Definition of punishment for certain acts of misconduct committed by servants or apprentices.

2. (1) Any servant or apprentice may be fined any sum not exceeding one pound sterling, and in default of payment of the same may be imprisoned, with or without hard labour, for any period not exceeding one month, in case he shall be convicted of any of the following acts or instances of misconduct, that is to say :

1. If he shall, after having entered into a contract, fail or refuse, without lawful cause, to commence the service at the stipulated time.
2. If he shall, without leave or other lawful cause, absent himself from his master's premises, or other place proper and appointed for the performance of his work.
3. If he shall, during working hours, unfit himself for the proper performance of his work by becoming or being intoxicated.
4. If he shall neglect to perform any work which it was his duty to have performed, or if he shall carelessly or improperly perform any work which from its nature, it was his duty, under his contract, to have performed carefully and properly.
5. If he shall, without leave and for his own purposes, make use of any horse, vehicle, or other property belonging to his master.

(1) Special J.P. has jurisdiction to try offences against this section. See § 22, Act 40, 1882 (Administration of Justice). See Act 30, 1889, *infra.*

Where a servant is accused of refusing to do his duty and desertion, he must be charged with contravening the appropriate sections of the statute which render these acts punishable offences.

A servant contravening sections 2 or 7 of the Act 18 of 1873 cannot on a first conviction be sentenced to imprisonment without the option of a fine. *Queen* v. *Police,* 2 E. D. C. 391. *Queen* v. *Jack,* 2 High Court. 587.

Spare diet cannot be imposed in the case of a first conviction for contravention of section 2 of Act 18 of 1873. *Queen* v. *Elsie Oliphant,* 5 E. D. C. 330. See also *Pentz* v. *Solomon & Co.,* Foord 52.

ᴵ. 6. If he shall refuse to obey any command of his master, or
of any person lawfully placed by his master in authority
over him, which command it was his duty to obey.

7. If he shall make any brawl or disturbance in or at his
master's dwelling-house, or on his master's farm, and
after being, by his master or any other person placed
by his master in authority over him, desired to desist,
shall, notwithstanding, continue making such brawl or
disturbance.

8. If he shall use any abusive or insulting language to his
master, or to his master's wife, or to any person placed
by his master in authority over him, calculated to
provoke a breach of the peace.

*Definition of punishment under either the next ensuing section
or the last preceding section in case of a second or further
conviction.*

3. (1) In case of a second conviction under the last preceding section, or of more such convictions than a second,
within the space of six months next after any former conviction,
the offender may, in regard to such second or any further
conviction, be fined any sum not exceeding three pounds
sterling, and in default of payment thereof may be imprisoned
and kept at hard labour for any period not exceeding six
weeks, and shall be liable during such imprisonment (or so
much thereof as the convicting magistrate shall adjudge) to
be kept in solitary confinement with or without spare diet, or
on spare diet with or without solitary confinement, subject as
hereafter is mentioned, and upon a conviction under the next
ensuing section of this Act followed within six months by a
conviction under the last preceding section, the offender shall
be liable to the like punishment, as if both convictions have
been had under the last preceding section.

*Definition of punishment for acts of misconduct of a more serious
nature committed by servants or apprentices.*

4. (1) Any servant or apprentice may be fined any sum not
exceeding three pounds sterling, and in default of payment,

(1) See Act 30, 1889, § 2, *infra.*

may be imprisoned, with or without hard labour, <u>for</u> any Act 18—1873. <u>period not exceeding two months,</u> or may be imprisoned <u>without the infliction of any fine,</u> at the discretion of the magistrate, with or without hard labour, for any period <u>not exceeding two months,</u> and during such imprisonment as in this section is mentioned, may be kept in solitary confinement with or without spare diet, or on spare diet with or without solitary confinement, subject as hereafter in the nineteenth section is mentioned, in case he shall be convicted in any of the following acts or instances of <u>misconduct,</u> that is to say :

1. If he shall by <u>wilful breach of duty, or</u> by neglect of duty, or through drunkenness, do any act tending to the immediate <u>loss, damage,</u> or serious risk of any property placed by his master in his charge, <u>or placed by any</u> other person in his charge for delivery to or on account of his master.

2. If he shall by <u>wilful breach of duty, (1) or by</u> neglect of duty, or through drunkenness, <u>refuse or omit to do any</u> lawful act proper and requisite to be done by him for preserving in safety any property placed by his master in his charge, or placed by any other person in his charge for delivery to or on account of his master.

3. If being employed as a <u>herdsman,</u> he shall fail to report to his master the death or loss of any animals placed in his charge, which he shall allege to have died or been lost, on the earliest opportunity for so doing after he shall have discovered or in the course of duty was bound to have discovered, such death or loss, or if he shall fail to preserve for his master's use or inspection any part or parts of any such animal as he shall allege to have died which part or parts he shall by his master have been directed to preserve, (2) unless such herdsman shall prove to the satisfaction of the court the death of such animals, or if it shall be made by his master to appear that any such animal or animals alleged by him to have strayed away or otherwise become irrecoverably

(1) A servant convicted under clause 2 of section 4 of Act No. 18 of 1873, of breach of duty whereby his master's property is lost, cannot be sentenced to imprisonment and to pay the value of the property lost. *Queen* v. *Whitbooy,* 2 E. D. C. 161.   (2) 1 Juta 409.

lost, could not, under the circumstances of the case, have become irrecoverably lost without his act or default.

4. If, being employed in any capacity other than that of a herdsman, he shall allege the loss of any property placed in his charge by or for his master, and it shall be made by his master to appear that the property in question could not have been lost without his act or default.

5. [Repealed by § 4, Act 7, 1875.]

6. (1) If he shall, without lawful cause, depart from his master's service, with intent not to return thereto.

Definition of punishment under either the last preceding section or the second section in cases of a second or further conviction.

5. (2) In case of a second conviction under the last preceding section, or of more such convictions than a second, within the space of six months next after any former conviction, the offender may, in regard to such second or any further conviction, be fined any sum not exceeding five pounds sterling, and in default of payment thereof may be imprisoned and kept at hard labour for any period not exceeding three months, or may be imprisoned, without the infliction of any fine, at the discretion of the magistrate, with or without hard labour, for any period not exceeding three months, and shall be liable during such imprisonment as in this section is mentioned, or so much thereof as the convicting magistrate shall adjudge, to be kept in solitary confinement, with or without spare diet, or on spare diet with or without solitary confinement, subject as hereafter mentioned; and upon a conviction under the second section of this Act, followed within six months by a conviction under the last preceding section, the offender shall be liable to the like punishment as if both convictions had been had under the last preceding section.

(1) See § 2, Act 7, 1875, *infra.*
(2) See Act 30, 1889, § 2, *infra.*

Act 18—1873.

No fine or imprisonment shall have the effect of cancelling
a contract.

6. (1) No fine paid or period of imprisonment undergone
under this Act by a servant or apprentice shall have the effect
of cancelling the contract of service or apprenticeship.

Certain exception from the second to sixth section, inclusive, and
the ninth section.—Provision for the punishment of servants
and apprentices other than those engaged in agriculture or
employed to work on farms.

7. (2) Nothing in any of the preceding sections from
second to sixth, both inclusive, nor in section nine, shall
extend or apply to servants or apprentices under the age of
sixteen years, or to servants or apprentices other than those
engaged in agriculture or employed to work on farms: Provided, however, that any servant or apprentice other than
those engaged in agriculture or employed to work on farms as
last mentioned, not being under sixteen years of age, may :

1. If he shall, after having entered into a contract, fail or
   refuse without lawful cause to commence the service at
   the stipulated time :

2. If he shall, without leave or other lawful cause, absent
   himself from his master's premises, or other place proper
   and appointed for the performance of his work : (3)

(1) See Act 30, 1889, § 2, *infra.*
(2) See note to § 2. See also Act 30, 1889, *infra.*
(3) In the case of *Roper v. Argus Printing and Publishing Company,*
heard on appeal in the Supreme Court on the 12th of April, 1889, from a
judgment of the Resident Magistrate of Cape Town, the summons set forth
that appellant by absenting himself from service between the 26th March and
the 1st April last had contravened the Masters and Servants Act. To this
the appellant (the defendant in the court below), before pleading took
exception, on the ground that a lithographic artist was not a servant within
the meaning of the Act, and therefore could not be summoned under such
Act. The exception was, however, overruled, and the Magistrate found the
defendant guilty, and sentenced him to pay a fine of 10s. or a week's
imprisonment in default. The whole case turned upon the question whether
or not a lithographic artist was a servant or handicraftsman. Counsel's
contention was that a lithographic artist like a reporter or an engraver was
not a servant, but a man who had an art function, and not the function of a

Act 18—1873.   3. If he shall, during working hours, unfit himself for the
proper performance of his work by becoming or being
intoxicated :

4. If he shall neglect to perform any work which it was his
duty to have performed, or if he shall carelessly or
improperly perform any work which from its nature it
was his duty, under his contract, to have performed
carefully and properly :

---

handicraftsman. It was quite open for Mr. Dormer to have taken action
against his client in another manner, instead of exposing him to fine or imprisonment. Counsel having addressed the court on behalf of the respondent,
urging that an artificer and a handicraftsman were in a very similar
position,

The Chief Justice said, from the record it appeared that the respondent
Dormer, in his capacity as managing director of the Argus Printing and
Publishing Company, engaged the appellant, Roper, in London, as a general
lithographic artist, for a term of three years. The agreement was made in
writing, and specified that Roper was to perform all such duties as might be
assigned to him in the general lithographic work of the establishment. When
Roper arrived in the colony, Roper ratified the agreement before the Magistrate
and took up his duties. Having noticed something in the papers about an
alteration in the constitution of the company, he absented himself from his
work, and was warned by Dormer to appear before the Magistrate to answer
a charge of having contravened paragraph 2 of section 7 of the Masters and
Servants Act. He was found guilty and fined, with the alternative of imprisonment. The ordinary law regarding contracts between masters and
servants did not give other than a civil remedy, but, owing to the circumstances
of the country, the Parliament had decreed that certain offences by servants
should be subjected to criminal penalties, when violations of contracts were
proved. He must say that the arguments on both sides had been particularly
interesting as well as able, and he had listened to them with a great deal of
attention, but the conclusion he had come to after giving the matter careful
consideration was that this was not a breach of contract which it was intended
by Parliament should be punished criminally. It could not, in his opinion,
be said that a person who came out from England, as a general lithographic
artist, to perform the duties specified in his contract, was a servant under the
definition of the Act. He did not think that Parliament intended the Act to
apply to cases of this kind, but to the more general contracts between masters
and servants, and he did not think that Roper in this case had rendered
himself liable, for his breach of contract with Dormer, to be taken before the
magistrate and punished criminally. On this sole ground he held that the
appellant was not a servant within the meaning of the Masters and Servants
Act. The appeal must therefore be allowed with costs, and the conviction
quashed. Roper was in the enjoyment of a very substantial salary, and
Dormer was not without his legal remedy.

5. If he shall, without leave or for his own purposes, make Act 18—1873. use of any horse, vehicle, or other property belonging to his master :

6. If he shall refuse to obey any command of his master, or of any person lawfully placed by his master in authority over him, which command it was his duty to obey :

7. If he shall by wilful breach of duty, or by neglect of duty, or through drunkenness, do any act tending to the immediate loss, damage, or serious risk of any property placed by his master in his charge, or placed by any other person in his charge for delivery to or on account of his master :

8. If he shall by wilful breach of duty, or by neglect of duty or through drunkenness refuse or omit to do any lawful act proper and requisite to be done by him for forwarding in safety any property placed by his master in his charge for delivery to or on account of his master :

9. (1) If he shall use any abusive or insulting language to his master, or to his master's wife, or to any person placed by his master in authority over him, calculated to provoke a breach of the peace :

be fined any sum not exceeding two pounds, and in default of payment be sentenced to be imprisoned for any period not exceeding one month ; but if it shall appear that such servant or apprentice is able to pay the damage caused by such act or default as in this section aforesaid, it shall be competent for the magistrate, whether the master shall agree thereto or not, to proceed under section thirteen, chapter five, of Act No. 15, 1856.

Complaints under foregoing sections to be lodged within one month.

8. No servant or apprentice shall be convicted under any of the foregoing sections of this Act unless the master shall lodge his complaint within one month next after the day on which he became cognizant of the offence or alleged offence.

(1) 9th paragraph added by Act 7 of 1875, *infra.*

Servant to appear before a magistrate on order of master, and failing to appear to be liable to expenses on conviction.

9. (1) In order to save time and expense, the master of any servant or apprentice alleging matter of complaint against such servant or apprentice may warn and order such servant or apprentice to appear before the magistrate of the district, on some day and hour to be named by such master, there to answer some certain charge, of the nature of which such complainant shall inform such defendant; and should the defendant fail to attend, in pursuance of such warning, the magistrate, upon the application of the complainant, and upon proof by affidavit that such defendant received such warning, and received the same a reasonable time before the time fixed for his appearance, and that to the best of the deponent's knowledge and belief, such defendant has no lawful cause for not appearing, may issue his warrant for the apprehension of such defendant, in order to the trial of the complaint ; and on such trial, and if the servant or apprentice shall be convicted of the offence with which he shall be charged, the magistrate may (if he shall be satisfied that the defendant had no good and sufficient cause for failing to attend), in addition to the punishment to which the defendant may be sentenced, adjudge the said defendant to pay to his master such reasonable costs and expenses, not being more than those allowed in criminal cases, to which his master may have been put in consequence of the defendant having failed to attend as aforesaid : Provided, always, that on issuing such warrant as aforesaid, the defendant shall be warned by summons to answer the charges brought against him, and to show cause why he shall not be adjudged to pay such expenses as aforesaid in consequence of his default in attendance.

Master having warned and ordered his servant to appear before a magistrate, upon failing to appear himself to be liable to expenses, and to penalties on failure to pay them.

10. Should any complainant who shall have warned any such defendant as aforesaid to appear as aforesaid himself fail

(1) See Act 30, 1889 §§ 2 and 3, *infra* (master may require servant to appear before special J.P.).

to appear at the time fixed by him for the appearance of such defendant then and there to prosecute his complaint, the magistrate, upon proof by affidavit that such defendant was warned by such complainant to appear at the said time to answer a charge of a certain nature, shall, unless satisfied that such complainant had a good and sufficient reason for failing to appear at such time, ascertain the distance which such defendant shall have travelled, and the distance which any person or persons shall have travelled whom such defendant shall have brought with him as witnesses, and shall, upon being satisfied that such witnesses would or might have been necessary for his defence, make an order in writing against such complainant for the payment of the expenses of such defendant and his witnesses, if any, at and after the same rate as if each of the said persons had been a witness summoned at the instance of the public prosecutor, and attending to give evidence in the court of such magistrate upon a criminal case ; and if such complainant shall, upon presentation to him of such order by the person or persons in whose favour the same shall have been made, refuse or neglect to comply therewith, he shall incur and be liable to a fine not exceeding five pounds sterling, and in default of payment of the same to imprisonment, with or without hard labour, for any period not exceeding one month : Provided that one such order may include the expenses of all or any of the persons whose expenses are to be paid, or separate orders may be delivered to one or more of such persons, as may be most convenient.

Servant or apprentice having complained against his master, failing to appear at time fixed to be liable to expenses, and to penalties on failure to pay them.

11. Should any servant or apprentice who shall have complained against his master for or on account of any offence against any of the provisions of this Act fail to appear at the time fixed by the magistrate for the appearance of the defendant, then and there to prosecute his complaint, the magistrate may, unless satisfied that such complainant had a good and sufficient reason for failing to appear at such time, ascertain in the manner in the last preceding section mentioned the expenses and costs which the defendant has

Act 18—1873. reasonably incurred in appearing to answer such complaint, and he shall in the manner in the last preceding section mentioned order the payment by the complainant of such costs and expenses ; and if, on the presentation to him of the order therein mentioned by the person in whose favour it is made, such complainant shall refuse or neglect to comply therewith, he shall incur and be liable to the same fine, and in default of payment thereof to the same punishment, as is fixed in the last preceding section : Provided that one such order may include the expenses of all or any of the persons whose expenses are to be paid, or separate orders may be delivered to one or more of such persons, as may be most convenient.

Servant or apprentice may leave his place of service to lodge complaint.

12. No servant or apprentice who shall leave the place of his service for the purpose merely of lodging any complaint which he may have against his master, after leave for that purpose shall have been unreasonably refused, shall by reason only of his so leaving be deemed to have deserted his master's service, or to have in any wise contravened this Act.

Servant or apprentice summoned under the second section may be found guilty under the fourth section and vice versâ.

13. A servant or apprentice summoned to answer for an offence alleged in the summons to be in contravention of the second section of this Act, should the proof given in the case show that he is guilty of contravening not the second but the fourth section of this Act, may be convicted and sentenced according to the evidence ; and, in like manner, a servant or apprentice summoned to answer for an offence alleged in the summons to be in contravention of the fourth section aforesaid, should the proof given show that he is guilty of contravening not the fourth but the said second section, may be convicted and sentenced according to the evidence : Provided, however, that the punishment to be awarded upon a conviction in either of these cases shall not exceed the punishment provided by the said second section : Provided, also, that the servant or apprentice shall have had in every case sufficient notice of the nature of the charge which he was called upon to answer.

Act 18—1873.

Definition of punishment for withholding wages by master.—
Judgment may be given for wages alone with or without
costs.

14. (1) As often as the master of any servant or apprentice
shall be convicted of the offence of withholding the wages of
such servant or apprentice without reasonable and probable
cause for believing that the wages so withheld were not really
due, he shall be fined any sum not exceeding five pounds
sterling, and in default of payment shall be imprisoned, for
any period not exceeding one month; and the convicting
magistrate shall, besides passing the said sentence, give
judgment for the amount of the wages so wrongfully withheld,
and for the costs of the proceedings, which costs shall be the
same as in a civil case before the said court; and the said
wages and costs shall, if not paid, be levied of the movable
property of the master, under and by virtue of a warrant under
the hand of the said magistrate, together with the cost of such
levy : Provided, however, that when and as often as the
magistrate shall acquit the master of the aforesaid offence, but
shall yet find that wages are due by such master to such
servant or apprentice which have been retained by such
master, it shall be lawful for such magistrate, and he is hereby
required, forthwith to give judgment for the amount of wages
which he shall find to be due to such servant, and make such
order as to the payment of costs, should he award any, by the
master, as shall seem to such magistrate to be in accordance
with real and substantial justice.

Definition of punishment for refusing to deliver servant's
property.—Penalty for default of payment of fine.

15. (2) As often as the master of any servant or apprentice
shall be convicted of the offence of having, either before or
after the expiration of the contract of service of apprenticeship, upon demand made and without lawful cause, refused to
deliver or permit to be taken away any of such servant's or
apprentice's cattle, sheep, goats, or other animals, lawfully

(1) *See* note (1) to sect. 2, Act 15, 1856, *supra.*
(2) *See also* Act 14, 1870 (Cattle Removal).

3. remaining or being upon such master's land without reasonable and probable cause for believing that the animals in question were lawfully detained, such master shall be fined any sum not exceeding one pound sterling for every animal so unlawfully detained; provided, however, that the total amount of a fine so payable shall not exceed the sum of five pounds sterling altogether; and in default of payment, shall be imprisoned for any period not exceeding one month; and the convicting magistrate shall, besides passing the said sentence, give judgment for the delivery of the said animals, and for costs, as in a civil action before the said court, which costs, if not paid, shall be levied in the same manner as in the fourteenth section directed; but the fact that the contract of service or apprenticeship of such servant or apprentice has not yet expired shall not be deemed or taken to be of itself reasonable or probable cause for such detention : Provided, however, that nothing herein contained shall impair the effect of any express contract of a lawful kind, by force of which the master shall claim a right to retain any such animals as aforesaid.

Definition of punishment for master failing to supply articles stipulated for in contract.

16. As often as the master of any servant or apprentice shall be convicted of the offence of failing, upon demand, to supply or deliver to such servant or apprentice the food, bedding, or other articles stipulated for in any written contract of service or apprenticeship, or of supplying or delivering food, bedding, or other articles not conformable to the said contract, he shall be liable to be fined any sum not exceeding five pounds sterling, and in default of payment to imprisonment for any period not exceeding one month.

Contract may be cancelled if the master has not faithfully performed his part thereof.

17. As often as it shall be made to appear to the magistrate, in any case instituted by any servant or apprentice against his master, that the master has not fairly and faithfully performed

his part of the contract of service or apprenticeship, the magistrate may, should he so think fit, and should the servant or apprentice so desire, order the cancellation of such contract of service or apprenticeship, and the same shall be cancelled accordingly.

Costs for compelling parties accused under this Act, and their witnesses, to attend the magistrate's court to be paid at the public charge under certain exceptions.—Penalties for bringing charge without reasonable cause.

18. As often as any master shall complain against his servant or apprentice, or any servant or apprentice shall complain against his master, for or on account of any offence against the provisions of this Act, the process of the court of the resident magistrate for compelling the attendance of the party accused and of all necessary witnesses shall be instituted at the public charge and without any fees of court : Provided always, that if at the trial the charge shall appear to have been brought without reasonable or probable cause, the party complaining shall be liable to a fine not exceeding five pounds, and also to defray the costs of process and of the witnesses in the case; and in default of payment of such fine and costs, shall be liable to be imprisoned for any period not exceeding one month; Provided, also, that such fine may be imposed upon the occasion of such trial, and without any fresh action or proceeding for the recovery thereof.

Regulations as to spare diet and solitary confinement.

19. In regard to the infliction of spare diet and solitary confinement under this Act, the resident magistrate shall observe and conform to such regulations and restrictions as shall have been or shall from time to time be issued by the Governor under the Act No. 20 of 1856.

Fines to be paid into Treasury.

20. All fines under this Act shall, when recovered, be paid into the public treasury.

Certain sections of Act 15 of 1856 repealed.

21. Sections 3, 4, 5, 6, 7, 8, 9, 16, 17, 18, 19, 20, 21, 22, 23, 25, and 26 of the fifth chapter, and so much of any other portion of Act No. 15 of 1856, as is inconsistent with or repugnant to any of the provisions of this Act, shall be and the same are hereby repealed.

Short title.

22. This Act may be cited for all purposes as the "Masters and Servants Law Amendment Act, 1873."

Act 28—1874. No. 28—1874.] ACT [July 31, 1874.

TO AMALGAMATE THE LAWS RELATING TO MASTERS, SERVANTS, AND APPRENTICES.

Preamble.

Whereas in several parts of the Act No. 15 of 1856, intituled "An Act to amend the Laws regulating the relative Rights and Duties of Masters, Servants, and Apprentices," reference is made to other parts of the said Act, and whereas many of these references have become inapplicable by reason of the repeal of the said Act by the "Masters and Servants Law Amendment Act, 1873," and it is desirable that the said two Acts should be read together: Be it enacted by the Governor of the Cape of Good Hope, with the advice and consent of the Legislative Council and the House of Assembly thereof, as follows:

Act No. 18 of 1873 to be construed with Act No. 15 of 1856.

1. The said "Masters and Servants Law Amendment Act, 1873," shall be construed with and as part of the said Act, No. 15 of 1856.

Short title.

2. This Act may be cited for all purposes as the "Masters and Servants Law Amalgamation Act, 1874," and the said Act No. 15 of 1856 may for all purposes be cited as the "Masters and Servants Law Act, 1856."

No. 7—1875.]   ACT   [June 30, 1875.

To Amend the Law relating to Masters, Servants, and Apprentices.

Preamble.

Whereas it is expedient to amend the law relating to Masters, Servants, and Apprentices: Be it enacted by the Governor of the Cape of Good Hope, with the advice and consent of the Legislative Council and House of Assembly thereof, as follows :

Servant or apprentice may be apprehended summarily on deposition of master.—Penalty for malicious depositions.

1. (1) If the master of any servant or apprentice alleging matter of complaint against such servant or apprentice for any offence punishable under the "Masters and Servants Law Act, 1856," or the "Masters and Servants Law Amendment Act, 1873," shall make deposition on oath before a resident magistrate, or justice of the peace, that he believes (stating the grounds of his belief) that in order to secure the appearance of such servant or apprentice before the resident magistrate having jurisdiction to try the case, that the apprehension of such servant or apprentice is necessary, it shall be lawful for such resident magistrate or justice of the peace to issue his warrant for the apprehension of such servant or apprentice without any previous warning or summons : Provided, how-

(1) *See* Act 30, 1889, sect. 3, *infra* (master may require servant to appear before Special J.P.).

E

Act 7—1875. ever, that if the master of any servant or apprentice shall make such deposition maliciously and without reasonable and probable ground for believing the same to be true, such master shall be liable to be fined any sum not exceeding five pounds, and in default of payment thereof to be imprisoned for any period not exceeding one month.

May be apprehended summarily for desertion.

2. If any servant or apprentice is charged under either of the aforesaid Acts with having, without lawful cause, departed from his master's service with intent not to return thereto, it shall be lawful for any resident magistrate or justice of the peace to issue his warrant for the apprehension of such servant or apprentice without any previous warning or summons.

Punishment for abusive language.

3. (1) There shall be considered as inserted in the seventh section of the said "Masters and Servants Law Amendment Act, 1873," after the paragraph of the said section numbered eight, the following as a ninth paragraph:

9. If he shall use any abusive or insulting language to his master, or to his master's wife, or to any person placed by his master in authority over him, calculated to provoke a breach of the peace.

Paragraph 5, section 4, Act 18, 1873, repealed.

4. The paragraph numbered five of the fourth section of the said last-mentioned Act is hereby repealed.

Accused competent to give evidence.

5. On the trial of any case in any court of resident magistrate wherein any master, servant, or apprentice is charged with having contravened any of the provisions of the said Masters and Servants Acts, such master, servant, or appren-

(1) *Vide* Act 30, 1889, *infra.*

tice, as the case may be, and his or her wife or husband, shall Act 7—1875. be competent, but not compellable, to give evidence on his or her own behalf, or on the behalf of the complainant in the said case.

Accused not compellable to enter the dock, but may be detained in custody.

6. No master, servant, or apprentice charged with having contravened any of the provisions of the said Masters and Servants Acts, and who is not immediately before the hearing of such charge in actual custody, shall be compelled to enter the dock or place usually assigned for prisoners under trial in the court, or shall be otherwise treated as under arrest, during the hearing of such charge : Provided that if, in the opinion of the magistrate before whom the charge is heard it shall be necessary, in order to secure the attendance of such master, servant, or apprentice, that he should be placed in custody, it shall be lawful for such magistrate to cause such person to be arrested and detained in custody.

Officer in charge of any public work may prosecute.

7. In case it may be necessary to prosecute or proceed against any person employed on any of the public works of this Colony for contravening any of the provisions of the said Masters and Servants Acts, such prosecution or proceeding may be carried on by and in the name of any of the officers in charge of the work upon which such servant is employed at the time of such contravention.

Short title.

8. This Act may be cited for all purposes as the " Masters and Servants Act, 1875," and shall be construed as one with the Masters and Servants Act, 1856, and the Act of 1873, amending the same ; and the said Acts, the Master and Servants Law Amalgamation Act, 1874, and this Act, may be cited collectively as the " Masters and Servants Acts, 1856 to 1875."

No. 30—1889.]   ACT   [August 13, 1889.

To Amend the Law relating to Masters, Servants, and Apprentices.

Be it enacted by the Governor of the Cape of Good Hope, by and with the advice and consent of the Legislative Council and House of Assembly thereof, as follows :

Special J.P.'s jurisdiction extended to all offences against Masters and Servants Acts.

1. Every Special Justice of the Peace shall, within the local limits by law fixed and determined for his jurisdiction, have and be entitled to exercise over and in respect of any person with regard to any offence wherewith such person shall be charged against any provision of any of the Acts commonly called the "Masters and Servants Acts, 1856 to 1875," as amended by this Act, the same jurisdiction, power and authority, as if he were a Resident Magistrate ; provided that it shall not be lawful for any such Special Justice of the Peace to punish any offender, subject to the provisions of the said Acts, in any higher or more severe manner than by fine, not exceeding two pounds, or by imprisonment, with or without hard labour, and with or without spare diet, and with or without solitary confinement, or either of them, for any period not exceeding one month : Provided, further, that the provisions of the third to the eleventh sections inclusive, and of the thirteenth section of the Act No. 10 of 1876 (1) shall *mutatis mutandis* apply to regulate, limit, and define the jurisdiction of and the procedure to be adopted by every Special Justice of the Peace under the authority of this section.

Offender against section 7 of Act 18, 1873, may be imprisoned without option of fine.

2. Notwithstanding anything to the contrary contained in the seventh section of the Act No. 18 of 1873 (2), as

(1) Special Justices of the Peace Act, p. 1308 of the new edition of the Statute Law.

(2) *Vide* p. 39, *supra*.

amended by the third section of the Act No. 7 of 1875 (1), the Act 30—1889. provisions of the second to the sixth sections inclusive and the ninth sections respectively of the said Act No. 18, 1873 (as the last-mentioned section is amended by this Act) shall extend and apply to any man-servant employed as a domestic servant or to perform any bodily labour in manufactures, or as a boatman, porter, groom, stablekeeper, gardener, or other occupation of a like nature.

Servant or apprentice reasonably suspected of offence against Masters and Servants Acts must accompany master before Magistrate ; if he refuses is liable to arrest.

3. Notwithstanding anything to the contrary contained in the ninth section of the Act No. 18 of 1873, or in the first section of the Act No. 7 of 1875, it shall be lawful for the master of any servant or apprentice, if he shall have reasonable and probable cause to suspect such servant or apprentice of having committed any offence against any provision of any of the Acts commonly called the " Masters and Servants Acts, 1856 to 1875," as amended by this Act, to order and require such servant or apprentice forthwith to proceed in his, the said master's, company before the nearest Resident Magistrate or Special Justice of the Peace having jurisdiction in the district or place where such master so suspects that such offence has been committed, there to answer a charge of having committed such offence ; and any servant or apprentice who shall neglect or refuse to obey any such order made by his master, having such reasonable and probable cause of suspicion as aforesaid, shall be liable to be arrested by his master without warrant, and conveyed in custody before such Resident Magistrate or Special Justice of the Peace as aforesaid, to be by him dealt with according to law ; provided that no servant or apprentice shall be bound or obliged to obey such order as aforesaid, unless or until he shall be informed of the nature of the charge which his master intends to prefer against him.

(1) *Vide* p. 50, *supra.*

Effect and short title of Act.

4. This Act may be cited for all purposes as the "Masters and Servants Act, 1889," and shall be construed as one with the "Masters and Servants Acts, 1856 to 1875," which, with this Act, may be cited collectively as the "Masters and Servants Acts, 1856 to 1889."

EMPLOYERS' LIABILITY.

No. 35—1886.]   ACT   [July 6, 1886.

To Extend and Regulate the Liability of Employers to make Compensation for Personal Injuries Suffered by Workmen in their Service.

Preamble.

Whereas the law relating to the Liability of Employers to make Compensation for Injuries suffered by Workmen in their Service is at present vague and uncertain, and it is desirable to amend the same, and to extend and regulate such liability : Be it therefore enacted by the Governor of the Cape of Good Hope, with the advice and consent of the Legislative Council and House of Assembly thereof, as follows :—

In what cases compensation to be made to injured workmen.

1. Whenever, after the taking effect of this Act, personal injury is caused to a workman :
   (1) By reason of any defect in the condition of the ways, works, machinery, or plant connected with, or used, in the business of the employer ; or
   (2) By reason of the negligence of the employer, or any person in the service of the employer who has any superintendence entrusted to him, whilst in the exercise of such superintendence ; or
   (3) By reason of the negligence of the employer, or any person in the service of the employer to whose orders

or directions the workman at the time of the injury was Act 35—1886.
bound to conform, and did conform, when such injury
resulted from his having so conformed ; or

(4) By reason of the act or omission of the employer, or any
person in the service of the employer done or made in
obedience to the rules or by-laws of the employer, or in
obedience to particular instructions given by any
person delegated with the authority of the employer in
that behalf; or

(5) By reason of the negligence of the employer, or any
person in the service of the employer who has the
charge or control of any signal, points, locomotive
engine, train upon a railway, or any machinery or
hauling gear in or about any mine, the workman or, in
case the injury results in death, the legal personal
representatives of the workman, and any person entitled
in case of death, shall have the same right of compensation and remedies against the employer as if the
workman had not been a workman of, nor in the service
of the employer, nor engaged in his work.

Exceptions to the provisions of the above section.

2. A workman shall not be entitled under this Act to any
right of compensation or remedy against the employer in any
of the following cases; that is to say,—

(1) Under sub-section one of section one of this Act, unless
the defect therein mentioned arose from, or had not
been, or had not been discovered or remedied owing to
the negligence of the employer or of some person in
the service of the employer, and entrusted by him with
the duty of seeing that the. ways, works, machinery, or
plant were in proper condition.

(2) Under sub-section four of section one of this Act unless
the injury resulted from some impropriety or defect in
the rules, by-laws, or instructions therein mentioned :
Provided always that in case any such rule or by-law
shall have been submitted to the Governor, and approved
of by him by notification in the *Gazette,* or in case such
rule or by-law shall be made under the provisions of

any Act of Parliament, it shall not be deemed for the purposes of this Act to be an improper or defective rule or by-law.

(3) In any case where the workman knew of the defect or negligence which caused his injury, and failed within a reasonable time to give, or cause to be given, information thereof to the employer, or to some person superior to himself in the service of the employer, unless he was aware that the employer or such superior already knew of the said defect or negligence.

Limit of sum recoverable as compensation.

3. The amount of compensation under this Act shall not exceed such sum as may be found to be equivalent to the estimated earnings, during the three years preceding the injury, of a person in the same grade employed during those years in the like employment, and in the district in which the workman is employed at the time of the injury.

No compensation recoverable under any other law as well as under this Act.

4. No workman, or representative of a workman, shall be entitled to recover compensation for any injury done to him under any other existing law in addition to the compensation to which he may be entitled under this Act.

Limit of time within which actions must be brought.

5. All actions under this Act shall be commenced within six months after the occurrence of the injury for which compensation is sought.

Definitions.

6. For the purposes of this Act, unless the context otherwise requires,—

The expression " person who has superintendence entrusted to him " means a person whose sole or principal duty is that of superintendence, and who is not ordinarily engaged in manual labour.

The expression " employer" includes a body of persons corporate or unincorporate.

Where Act to be in force and Short Title.

7. This Act shall take effect only within such mining areas as the Governor may from time to time declare by Proclamation to be published in the *Gazette*, and may be cited as the "Employers' Liability Act, 1886."

TRADE BEYOND BOUNDARIES.

No. 81.]   [December 23, 1830.

Penalty on bringing natives into the colony against their free will, £100.—Agreement beyond the boundaries of the colony void.

12. And be it further enacted that it shall not be lawful for any person whomsoever to bring within this colony any person from beyond the said boundaries thereof not legally contracted to him within the colony, against the free will and consent of such person, under a penalty not exceeding one hundred pounds, and if any such person be brought within the colony upon any contract or agreement of any nature soever entered into beyond the said boundaries such contract or agreement shall be void and of no effect.

Legal contract before clerk of the peace of persons coming voluntarily into the colony.

13. Provided always, that nothing herein contained shall extend to prevent any native or other person who may have voluntarily come into the colony with or been brought by any trader or other person from entering into any legal contract or agreement before a clerk of the peace or other person before whom the same may be made.

No. 22—1857.]   AN ACT   [June 29, 1857.

For more effectually preventing the improper intro-
duction into this Colony of Children belonging to
Native Tribes resident in Territories beyond the
Land Boundaries thereof.

Preamble.

WHEREAS in some instances, persons visiting the territories
lying beyond the land boundaries of this colony have there
procured, and have thence brought into the colony, to be made
servants of, children of tender age, belonging to native tribes
resident in the territories aforesaid: And whereas there is
reason to believe that if the practice of procuring such children
were suffered to grow up, evil consequences may arise therefrom: And whereas the existing laws of the colony do not
sufficiently provide against the introduction of such children,
under such circumstances: Be it therefore enacted by the
Governor of the Cape of Good Hope, with the advice and
consent of the Legislative Council and House of Assembly
thereof, as follows:

*Native children under sixteen years of age not to be brought
within the colonial land boundary without previous sanction
of the Governor.—Except by the parent of the child or by
persons delivering the same to a resident magistrate within
fourteen days.—Such child to be under the guardianship of
the Governor and may not be apprenticed to the person by
whom it is brought in.—Children may accompany visitors
from beyond the land boundary for a temporary purpose upon
a certificate from a competent authority.—Any resident
magistrate receiving such certificate to note the date of its
production.*

1. No person, except as hereinafter excepted, shall, without
the previous sanction of the Governor of this colony for the
time being, first had and obtained, bring into this colony,
across the land boundary thereof, any child under the age of
sixteen years, belonging to any native tribe or people in Africa,

resident beyond the said land boundary. Any person con- Act 22—1857
travening this section of this Act shall, upon conviction, be
liable, for and in respect of every child so brought into this
colony, to a fine not exceeding twenty pounds, together with,
and in addition to, the sum of one shilling per day for every
day during which any such child shall have been harboured
or kept by such person within this colony : Provided that
nothing in this section contained shall extend to any parent of
any such child as aforesaid, lawfully entering this colony, and
bringing such child into the same, nor to any person whomsoever bringing into the colony any such child as aforesaid,
who shall deliver over such child to any resident magistrate
of the colony within the space of fourteen days next after the
day upon which such child shall have been brought into the
colony : Provided, however, that every such last-mentioned
child shall be placed under the guardianship of the Governor
of the colony, for the time being, as in the fifth section of this
Act provided, and that no such child shall be apprenticed to
or left with the person by whom such child shall have been
brought into the colony, as in the sixth section of this Act
provided : Provided, also, that nothing herein contained shall
apply to any inhabitant of any territory beyond the land
boundaries of this colony, visiting this colony for a temporary
purpose, and bringing into this colony any such child or
children as aforesaid, in case such inhabitant shall produce and
exhibit to some resident magistrate of this colony, within one
calendar month next after the date of his arrival in this colony,
a certificate in writing, signed by some magistrate of the
territory in which such inhabitant usually resides, certifying
that the child or children brought into the colony by such
person is or are lawfully in the service of such person, and that
the services of such child or children are required by such
person during or upon his journey : Provided, also, that the
resident magistrate to whom such certificate shall be produced
or exhibited shall endorse thereon the date at which the same
was so produced to him.

Penalty for keeping or harbouring any child brought into this colony in contravention of the last preceding section.

2. If any child brought by any person into this colony, in contravention of the last preceding section, shall, without the previous sanction of the Governor of this colony for the time being, be received, kept, or harboured, whilst under the age of sixteen years, by any other person within this colony, such last-mentioned person knowing, when so receiving, keeping, or harbouring such child, that such child had been brought into this colony, without the previous sanction of the said Governor, from beyond the land boundary thereof, then such last-mentioned person shall, upon conviction, be liable to the same penalty as that in the last preceding section mentioned : And any person receiving, keeping, or harbouring, within this colony, any child brought into this colony by any such inhabitant of another territory, as in the first section mentioned, shall be liable to the same penalty.

How to judge of the age of such children.

3. In every prosecution for a contravention of any of the sections of this Act, the court in which such prosecution shall be pending shall judge from the appearance of the child in question in such prosecution, and also, if needful, from the opinions, given under oath, of persons skilled in ascertaining the age of such children, and from any other evidence which may be adduced on the subject, whether the child referred to in such prosecution was, when brought into this colony, or received, kept, or harboured therein (as the case may be), under the age of sixteen years or not.

How to judge of the age if child has died.

4. When by reason of the death of such child, before the hearing of such criminal case as aforesaid, or other cause, the court in which such case shall be pending shall be unable to inspect the child in question, in such case, then such court shall judge of the age of such child when it was brought into

the colony, or received, kept, or harboured therein (as the case Act 22—1857 may be), by the knowledge or opinion of persons acquainted with such child.

Every child brought into the colony in contravention of the first section, placed under the guardianship of the Governor, and may be apprenticed or placed at an industrial school.— Guardianship not to extend beyond the age of eighteen.

5. Every child brought into this colony in contravention of the first section of this Act, whether the person who brought such child into the colony be convicted or not, and every child brought into this colony, by any inhabitant of another territory, as in the first section mentioned, which child shall be received, kept, or harboured by any other person within this colony, is hereby placed under the guardianship of the Governor of the colony for the time being, and may, by any person acting under the authority of the said Governor, be apprenticed in like manner as is, or shall be, by law provided in regard to destitute children, or the said Governor may, without, or before apprenticing such child, cause such child to be placed at any industrial school within this colony, and to be there maintained and instructed so long as may be necessary, or as the said Governor shall think fit : Provided that the guardianship of the Governor aforesaid shall not extend to, nor shall he cause to be apprenticed, or placed at an industrial school as aforesaid, any person who shall be of the age of eighteen years or upwards.

No such child to be apprenticed or left with the person by whom introduced or harboured in the colony.

6. No such child as aforesaid shall, in any case, be apprenticed to or left with the person by whom, in contravention of the first section of this Act, such child was brought into this colony, or any person by whom, in contravention of the second section of this Act, such child was received, kept, or harboured, after being brought into this colony.

[The remaining sections of this Act relate to children brought into the Colony prior to its promulgation, and have no further applicability.]

PRESCRIPTION (DEBTS) ACT.

No. 6—1861.]   [August 14, 1861.

Prescription of three years established in certain cases.

5. No suit or action for the fees or for the fees and disbursements of advocates, attorneys, public notaries, conveyancers, land surveyors, or persons practising any branch of the medical profession, or for the amount of any baker's, or butcher's, or tailor's, or dressmaker's, or boot and shoemaker's bill or account,—nor any suit or action for the salary or wages of any merchant's clerk or other persons employed in any merchant's or dealer's store, counting-house, or shop, —nor any suit or action for the wages as a servant of any person coming under the definition of the term "servant" given in the Masters and Servants Act, No. 15 of 1856, shall (except as hereinafter is excepted) be capable of being brought at any time after the expiration of three years from the time when the cause of action in any such case as aforesaid first accrued or in case such cause or action shall have already accrued, then after the expiration of three years from the time of the taking effect of this Act : Provided that as often as any acknowledgment of or promise in writing to pay any such debt as is in this section mentioned, shall have been made or given at any time before the expiration of such term of three years, then such debt may be sued for at any time within eight years from the date of such acknowledgment or promise, or in case such acknowledgment or promise shall specify some future time for the payment of the debt, then within eight years from the date at which the said debt became, by or according to the tenor or effect of such acknowledgment or promise, due and payable.   And provided that nothing in this section contained shall prevent the application to any such debt as is in this section mentioned of any of the provisions of the eighth section of this Act.

How in regard to minors or persons under legal disability.

6. If at the time when any such cause of action as is in the second, third, and fifth sections of this Act mentioned,

first accrued, the person to whom the same accrued shall Act 6—1861. have been a minor, or under coverture, or of unsound mind, or absent from the colony, then such person, or the person claiming through him may, notwithstanding that the period of prescription hereinbefore limited in regard to such cause of action shall have expired, bring a suit or action upon such cause of action at any time within eight years or three years (as the case may be) next after the time at which the person to whom such cause of action first accrued shall have ceased to be under any such disability as aforesaid, or shall have died, whichever of these two events shall have first happened.

PASSES TO NATIVES.

No. 22—1867.]   [August 16, 1867. Act 22—1867

Contracts under Masters and Servants Act to hold good.—But not to protect person infringing subsequent provisions of Act.

2. From and after the passing of this Act all contracts of service made between employers and natives or native foreigners, in conformity with the provisions of the Act No. 15 of the year 1856, commonly known as the "Masters and Servants Act," shall be good and valid in law; but the existence of any such contract shall not be allowed to protect any native foreigner who may be a party thereto from being prosecuted and punished for entering or being within the Colony without a pass, as hereinafter provided.

CATTLE REMOVAL ACT.

No. 14—1870.]   [May 5, 1870.

Certificate for removal of stock to be obtained.

2. It shall be the duty of every person desiring the removal of stock (1) from any place to any other place (2) to procure a certificate (3), signed by any resident magistrate, justice of the peace, field-cornet, or landholder, stating the date upon which the same is granted, the name of the owner, and the number and description of the stock to be removed, the name of the place from which the same is being removed, and of the place to which it is being sent; and also the name or names of the driver or drivers thereof.

Duty of landholder to grant certificate for removal of stock from his land.—How, if landholder refuses.

3. It shall be the duty of any landowner to grant, free of charge, such certificate as aforesaid, written in such language, whether English, Dutch, or native, as such landholder may be able to write intelligibly, to any person who, being in the lawful possession of any stock, desires to remove the same from land occupied by such landholder; and the refusal by

(1) "'Stock' shall mean any horse, gelding, mare, colt, filly, mule, or ass, or any bull, ox, cow, heifer, or calf, or any sheep or goat: Provided that stock under saddle, or pack-saddle, cattle employed in drawing any vehicle, whether inspanned or outspanned, or stock in the possession of the police shall not be deemed to be stock within the meaning of this Act," § 13, Act 14, 1870. No stock deemed to be removed merely by reason of their moving from place to place on land in which owner of stock has an interest or ownership, § 6, Act 20, 1889.

(2) Printed as amended by Act 20 of 1889.

(3) This Act to come into force or be suspended in any division, at the request of the Divisional Council of such division, by proclamation in the *Gazette*. Certificates, however, granted in places where Act not in force to be valid in any division where the law has been proclaimed, and when so proclaimed the 3rd and 4th sections to apply to the whole Colony, § 14, Act 14, 1870. A penalty of six months' imprisonment, with or without hard labour, may be imposed upon any one granting a false certificate or fraudulently altering one, § 12, Act 14, 1870.

the master of any servant or apprentice to grant, in regard to Act 14—1870. any stock of such servant or apprentice lawfully running or being upon the land of the said master, such a certificate as is in this Act mentioned, shall be deemed and taken to be, for the purpose of the twenty-first (1) section of chapter 5 of the Act No. 15, 1856, commonly called the Masters and Servants Act, a refusal by such master to deliver such stock or to permit the same to be taken away; and the provisions of the said twenty-first section shall apply to such case as fully as if the same were herein again set forth.

Who required to grant certificates.

4. It shall be the duty of any magistrate, justice of the peace, field-cornet, or landholder, to whom application is made for such certificate as aforesaid, to grant a certificate, written in such language, whether English, Dutch, or native, as the person applied to may be able to write intelligibly, to the person applying for the same : Provided that the magistrate, justice of the peace, field-cornet, or landholder to whom application is made shall be satisfied that the stock for the removal of which the certificate is required are the property or in the lawful possession of the person about to remove the same.

Persons driving stock may be required to produce certificate.—On failure to produce, &c., stock may be seized and impounded.

5. (2) It shall be lawful for any magistrate, justice of the peace, field-cornet, police officer, constable, or landholder, who shall find any person driving stock, to call upon such person to produce such certificate as aforesaid, and if such person shall fail to produce such certificate, or if the stock being removed shall not correspond in all material respects with the certificate produced, or if the direction in which such

(1) This section is repealed by § 21, Act 18, 1873, but see § 15 of latter Act.

(2) Person driving stock may be arrested without warrant, § 2, Act 20, 1889, and detained pending inquiry for not more than 4 weeks; *vide* § 3 of latter Act.

Act 14—1870. person is proceeding with the stock shall not correspond with the direction indicated in such certificate, or if the name of the person driving the stock shall not correspond with that in the certificate, then such magistrate, justice of the peace, field-cornet, police officer, constable, or landholder, if he shall be able to read such certificate (1), may take possession of such stock and cause the same to be conveyed to the nearest pound, there to remain until liberated by order of the resident magistrate, or otherwise disposed of as hereinafter provided.

REFORMATORY INSTITUTIONS.

Act 7—1879. No. 7—1879.]   [January 27, 1882.

Convicted child may be sentenced to detention in institution in addition to imprisonment.—Or may be sent to institution in lieu of imprisonment.

4. (2) Whenever any child shall hereafter be convicted of any offence, either upon indictment or on summary conviction punishable by imprisonment, it shall be lawful for the judge or other competent court by which such child shall be convicted, in addition to the sentence which may then and there be passed as a punishment for the said offence, to direct such child to be sent, at the expiration of such sentence, to any reformatory institution established under this Act, to be there detained until he or she reaches the age of sixteen years; or for such shorter period as such judge or other competent court may think fit; or such judge or other competent court may, if such judge or court deem fit, send such child to any reformatory institution in lieu and instead of sentencing such child to imprisonment, or may, at the expiration of any sentence, or instead of sentencing such child to imprisonment, order that such child shall be bound to some useful calling or occupation for such period as such judge or court shall think fit, but

(1) Printed as amended by Act 20 of 1889.
(2) See Act 8, 1889, *infra*.

not longer, however, than until such child shall attain the age of sixteen years.

Power to bind inmate as apprentice.

11. At any time before the expiration of the warrant authorising the detention of any inmate in a reformatory institution, the resident magistrate of the district in which such institution is situate, or of the district in which such child shall then be detained, may bind any such inmate as apprentice to any useful calling or occupation as he may think fit, in the same manner in which destitute children (1) are now authorised to be bound by the law of this colony; and such binding shall be as effectual as if such child were of full age and had bound himself: Provided that, if such child should have one or more parents or guardians alive, no such apprenticeship shall take place without the consent of such parents or guardians.

Provisions of articles of apprenticeship.

12. The resident magistrate may, in any articles of apprenticeship under this Act, provide that such portion of the wages to become due to such apprentice as he may think fit, shall be deposited, at such times and in such manner as he shall determine, in any savings or other bank of this colony on account of such apprentice, and every such deposit shall be deemed and allowed as a payment to such apprentice, but no portion thereof shall be withdrawn by such apprentice, without the consent in writing of such resident magistrate, until the expiration of the apprenticeship.

Apprentices absconding.—Penalties.

20. If any child apprenticed or bound under the provisions of this Act shall desert or abscond from the service of his master, it shall be lawful for any court before whom such apprentice shall be brought, upon proof to the satisfaction of such court, in addition to any punishment which may be

---

(1) See Act 15, 1856, § 6, *supra.*

Act 7—1879. inflicted, either to order the child to return to the service of such master, or that such child shall be detained in any reformatory institution until such child shall attain the age of sixteen years, or for any shorter period.

Accessories to escape or absconding.

21. Any person who shall directly or indirectly counsel or induce, by letter or otherwise, any inmate of any reformatory institution to abscond or escape therefrom, or break his apprenticeship and abscond from his master, before such inmate shall have been regularly discharged or before the expiration of such apprenticeship, or who shall aid or abet any such inmate in absconding or escaping, or who knowing such inmate to have absconded or escaped, shall harbour or conceal, or assist in harbouring or concealing, such inmate, or prevent him or her from returning to such reformatory institution, or to his master shall, on conviction thereof, forfeit and pay any sum not exceeding twenty pounds, or at the discretion of the court before which such conviction shall be had, be imprisoned for any term not exceeding six months, and with or without hard labour.

Act 8—1889. No. 8—1889.]   ACT   [June 28, 1889.

To Make further provision for the Apprenticeship of Juvenile Offenders.

Be it enacted by the Governor of the Cape of Good Hope, with the advice and consent of the Legislative Council and House of Assembly thereof, as follows:—

Juvenile offenders may be apprenticed until 21 years of age.

1. Whenever any child under the age of sixteen years shall be convicted of any offence in terms of the fourth section of the Reformatory Institutions Act, 1879, it shall be lawful for the court before which such conviction shall take place to

direct that, in lieu of any of the punishments in the said section mentioned, such child shall be apprenticed to some fit and proper person, who shall be willing to instruct and employ such child in some useful calling, trade, or other occupation, including domestic service and service as a farm labourer, until such child shall have attained his twenty-first year or for some shorter period.

Act 8—1889.

Act 15 of 1856 to apply.

2. All and singular the provisions of Act No. 15 ot 1856, relating to apprentices, save and except such provisions as are repugnant to or inconsistent with the provisions of this Act, shall, in so far as they are applicable, apply to persons directed to be apprenticed under this Act.

Contract executed before Resident Magistrate.

3. It shall be lawful for any Judge of the Supreme Court, before whom any child shall be convicted as aforesaid, to direct that the contract of apprenticeship shall be executed before a Resident Magistrate to be nominated by such Judge.

Resident Magistrates to be tutors of all minors apprenticed under this Act.

4. The Resident Magistrates of the Colony shall be *ex officio* the tutors of all minors apprenticed under this Act and residing within their respective districts instead of their parents, or tutors, testamentary or dative, and shall, upon proof of the unfitness, inability or unwillingness of any master to retain the custody of any such minor, cancel the contract of apprenticeship and apprentice the minor to some other fit and proper person.

Wages to be deposited in Savings Bank.

5. Whenever any wages shall be payable to any minor apprenticed under this Act such wages shall be deposited in his name in such Post Office Savings Bank as the Magistrate

shall direct, and shall not be handed over to such minor until the lawful expiration of his apprenticeship, unless the Magistrate shall for special reasons otherwise direct.

How apprentice may be transferred to another person.

6. No master shall assign or transfer to any other person any minor apprenticed under this Act without the consent of the Resident Magistrate of the district in which such master shall reside, but the consent of the minor or of his parents shall not be necessary.

Punishment of apprentice for deserting from service.

7. Any minor apprenticed under this Act who shall desert from his master's service during his term of apprenticeship shall be liable, upon conviction before any Court of Resident Magistrate, to be imprisoned with or without hard labour for any period not exceeding twelve months, or to receive twenty cuts with a cane, or to both such imprisonment and whipping.

How contract may be cancelled.

8. It shall be lawful for the Supreme Court, Eastern Districts Court, or High Court of Griqualand or any Circuit Court, within their respective jurisdictions, upon the application of any minor apprenticed under this Act, or of any parent or relative within the fourth degree of consanguinity of such minor, to order the cancellation of any such contract of apprenticeship, as aforesaid, and, if need be, to direct a fresh contract to be entered into before such Magistrate as shall be nominated by such court.

Inquiry as to fitness of master.—Notice to be given for applications.

9. Every Resident Magistrate shall, before approving of any contract of apprenticeship, make full inquiry as to the fitness of any master to whom the minor is proposed to be apprenticed, and may by advertisement in the *Gazette* and some news-

paper circulating in his district, give notice in the English Act 8—1889. and Dutch languages, that applications may be made to him by farmers and other persons wishing to have the convicted offender apprenticed to them. Such notice shall state the name and age of the offender, the offence of which he stands convicted, and the day upon which such applications will be heard before such magistrate.

Detention of offender until apprenticed.

10. It shall be lawful for the Resident Magistrate, pending the publication of such notice or pending such inquiry as in the last preceding section mentioned, whether the offender shall have been tried before him or shall have been sent by some Judge of the Supreme Court to be apprenticed by him, to direct that such offender shall be detained in prison or be admitted on bail until the contract shall be finally executed.

Short title.

11. This Act may be cited for all purposes as the " Juvenile Offenders Apprenticeship Act, 1889."

INDEX.

www.ingramcontent.com/pod-product-compliance
Lightning Source LLC
Chambersburg PA
CBHW031447270326
41930CB00007B/897